SCANDINAVIAN HUMOR & OTHER MYTHS

ANDERSON

NORDBOOK

For Adaire,
The Love of my Life
Who often thinks I am
very funny.

John Louis Anderson is a good Norwegian/Swedish/American boy who grew up in New Ulm, Minnesota, attended a good Lutheran college (Augustana, Sioux Falls), and got his M.A. from the University of Minnesota in Theatre Photography. He has worked as a photographer for the Guthrie Theatre, Chanhassen Theatre, and a number of national magazines in both the United States and Scandinavia.

He has written about Scandinavia and other topics for MPLS/ST.PAUL magazine, *Minnesota Monthly, Minneapolis Star & Tribune Travel Section*, and WCCO Radio.

The ladies on the cover are matriarchs of his extended family.

The New Scandinavian Gods first appeared in MPLS/ST. PAUL magazine.

First Printing .... June 1986
Sixth Printing .... February 1988

Published by
NORDBOOK
P.O.Box 6456
Minneapolis, MN 55406

Library of Congress Cataloging in Publication Data

Anderson, John Louis
Scandinavian Humor & Other Myths
1 United States - Social Life and customs-
-Anecdotes, facetiae, satire, etc.

ISBN O-9616967-0-2

Text, photography and hand tinting: John Louis Anderson
Editor: Sylvia Paine
Cover and Text design: Evans-Smith & Skubic, Inc.

TABLE OF CONTENTS

THE NEW SCANDINAVIAN GODS:

Cheap Cosmological Excuses for Why Scandinavian/Americans Behave the Way We Do.

Anybody who has ever had to live, work, or deal with Scandinavian/Americans notices the deep and pervasive cultural differences between us and the rest of the world. It's not just superficial oddities like an entire house full of blonde wood, or the odd nordic notion that herring is an appropriate breakfast food.

Some people are actually frightened of us. They don't necessarily feel safe around people who willingly ingest Lutefisk. These people need to understand our history.

Nearly a millennium ago, when the first missionaries came to the Scandinavian peninsula, they found that the Vikings worshiped such gods and goddesses as Thor, Odin, Freyja, and Sif. These deities possessed attributes much admired in those days: They knew how to weave thick clothes to avoid freezing to death, hit people hard on the head, went crazy in battle, and so on.

But these old gods have fallen into idleness and today are known only to Wagnerian opera buffs and Icelandic scholars. Theologians may debate how this old system and its unusual world view may have affected the development of Lutheranism, but its impact cannot be denied.

Beyond Lutheranism, there is a complex system of secret beliefs which shape our lives and dictate our actions. This secret code is so fundamental to Scandinavian/American life that it has, through the centuries, become encoded into our genetic code, tucked right up there on the DNA next to the bit about the blonde hair and blue eyes. The expression of this system—relying on neither the right nor the left hemisphere of the brain, but rather on the brain stem and spinal column—is shown in this series of updated nordic deities.

Non-Scandinavians who are desperately seeking explanations for our often baffling behaviors will find some answers here.

Scandinavians who wish to break free of their past and eat Jalapeno peppers without guilt can, perhaps, find courage through self-knowledge. Then again, maybe they can't.

COMATOSE
God of Fishing

No sport has attracted the following among Scandinavian/Americans that fishing has, and for good practical and theological reasons. First, all other sports require a lot of talking, running, or throwing things. Second, that state which other cultures and religions call nirvana—the condition of being at complete oneness with one's environment—is achieved by the Scandinavian only while fishing. Only fishing offers the perfect transcendental state: absolute silence (for lack of anything interesting to talk about), absolute motionlessness (rivaled only by rigor mortis) and a total intellectual and sensory deprivation (broken only by mosquitoes).

THERAPY
Goddess of Rosemaled Toilet Seats

It only stands to reason that in a culture that produced Danish design, Ibsen's and Strindberg's plays, Munch's paintings, Bergman's films and Aalto's buildings, there would be an artistic backlash. There is no other way to account for all the wooden horses, straw goats, painted sauna plaques, "Uff Da" buttons, wall hangings, bumper stickers and greeting cards. To say nothing of the rosemaling or dala painting on every surface that will accept paint.

What generally is not understood is the valuable role Therapy and her arts and crafts play in the well-being and survival of the Scandinavian community. In the enforced isolation of the winter months, she compels many people to make clever things with yarn, string, thread, or anything else that the more sensitive souls might otherwise use to hang themselves out of boredom and desperation.

Therapy is the guardian of sets of annual Christmas plates and any homemade thing that hangs on a kitchen wall.

CONVOLU
God of Sullen Depression

Scholars are virtually unanimous in their assessment of Convolu as the chief god of the New Nordic Cosmology. By way of proof, they point to his month-long festival of depression, known to us as January.

The month is universally started hung over from New Year's Eve and overweight from Christmas. No one can be pleasant on a diet of Ry-Krisp and cottage cheese. In an annual festival that has come to be known as "The Dance of the Brass Monkeys," the faithful gather at the International Falls, Minnesota weather station to chant:

"January in Minnesota
averages 11.2° F.
But in Reykjavik, Iceland,
it averages
31.4° F all January!
Oh, damn, am I cold!

All the Christmas lights are down, the snow is crusty and brown, and the Vikings aren't in the Super Bowl again. Then comes Convolu's major feast day—The Arrival of the Dayton's Bill. Even the arrival of the IRS forms is less vexing than the arrival of the Dayton's bill, because most people can expect a refund on their taxes, but the Dayton's bill sends all pretense of solvency out the window. All restaurants, theatres and nightclubs close for the night while the populace wails, pisses and moans. After that, they all feel much better, and the border attendants allow residents to check out for short periods when accompanied by an out-of-state relative.

LEFSE
Goddess of Unseasoned Food

The first time non-Scandinavians eat at a Scandinavian/American's house, they have the lingering suspicion that if they hadn't arrived so early, the cook would have had time to finish seasoning the food. What they don't realize is that the cook not only finished, but in honor of the new guests, probably doubled the spices.

To understand this culinary cult of blandness, one must recall that traditional Nordic peasants had a surplus of only one food—herring. It was even used somewhat indelicately for fertilizer in the fields. You cannot believe how difficult it is to find novel ways of seasoning your 17,528th meal of herring and potatoes; at some point you just throw your hands up in the air and bury it all under a mound of salt. Salt, and more aquavit. When the Scandinavians came to this country, they couldn't get much aquavit, so they stuck to their salt shakers.

Most Scandinavian food is classified as a "carrier." That is, it exists to carry something else down your gullet—usually something better-tasting. Lefse carries sugar, boiled potatoes carry salt, and even lutefisk (I am told) can be made sufferable if it can be made to carry enough butter.

Lefse, the Goddess of Unseasoned Food, is venerated wherever casseroles are called hot dishes.

FRIGIDAIRE
Goddess of Eroticism
and her consort,
TEPID
God of Personal Space

Nothing is more widespread than the myth of the Sex Maniac Scandinavian, and nothing is more baffling to those who have actual daily contact with Scandinavians.

Under the influence of Frigidaire and Tepid, Scandinavian/Americans have developed a complex approach/avoidance set of behaviors. Under Frigidaire's influence, a Scandinavian/American's wild and crazy side only comes out when the situation makes it impossible to act on the impulse. A recent poll of Scandinavian/Americans showed that many see themselves as "Most likely to get romantic" during: 1) the start of a nonstop flight to the Far East, 2) A Luther League meeting, and 3) A family reunion.

As for Tepid's side of this equation, most people polled said they were "Likely to have a headache:" 1) During Johnny Carson's show, 2) After a play at the Guthrie, with a fancy, intimate dinner beforehand, or 3) During a moonlit stroll through the woods.

The roles of Frigidaire and Tepid are not gender-specific, and are interchangeable between partners. The only danger is if both partners assume the same role. At one extreme, blondes could become an endangered species. At the other, more ground could be torn up than during a snowmobile race in a snowless winter.

NO WAY
God of Suspicion

Scandinavians have a tradition of suspicion and skepticism that derives directly from the ancient cult of No Way. Despite recent attempts to prove otherwise (most notable Prof. C. F. Sweedlund's fatuous monograph, "Grinning and Other Signs of Civility among Late-Bronze Age Scandinavian Peninsular Peoples"), we know for a fact that the Vikings used to sulk and argue for hours before deciding whether to get off the boat and sack the town in front of them.

It usually went like this: First, Ragnar the Old Poop would argue that they hardly knew these people—what if they laughed at them? Then Eyolf the Scowler would interrupt, saying he didn't want anything to do with anyone he hadn't known for years. Eric the Irritated would finally start shouting that the tide was going out, and if they didn't do something quick they'd have nothing left to raid except the farm on the point, and they'd have gone all the way to France and come home with nothing but a bunch of damned wool again. That would make Knut the Pouter grab the tiller and shout, "That does it! I don't care! I'm turning this boat around right now if you guys can't make a simple decision!"

INCLEMENT
God of School Closings

The best-known god to non-Scandinavians is Inclement. Often the only thing people on the coasts and in foreign countries know about Minnesota is that we've got really awful weather. What they don't know is why we stay.

We stay because we love to be around during March. At a time when everybody else in the country is flying kites, we are having the snowiest month of the year. The radio stations stop announcing school closings and instead read the names of those schools still open. The temptation to escape to Mardi Gras dissipates when you find you can't get out because the airport is snowed in. Every Minnesota newspaper and several papers nationwide carry the picture and story of the lady who delivers her baby on the back of a snowmobile while bounding through the drifts to the hospital.

Old timers contend that nature's rhythms have been upset by the girl's state high-school basketball tournament. Not knowing until the last minute which week to deliver its annual Tournament Blizzard, it blizzards during both the boys' and the girls' tournaments.

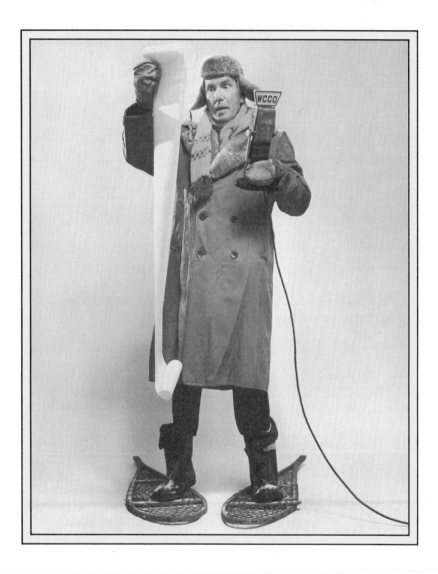

TACIT
God of Keeping It to Yourself

Scandinavians have a gift for making Calvin Coolidge and Trappist monks look like babbling, chattering, nonstop talkers. This is not surprising in a culture that puts so high a premium on keeping everything to yourself. Other nationalities have variously interpreted the Nordic's natural reticence as autism, hostility, ignorance, arrogance, and sub-clinical depression. Since very few people exhibit *all* of these characteristics, it would seem that these theories are on somewhat shaky ground.

Pastor N.S. Haggstrom got such a good response to his sermon, "God Knows Everything, So Why Are You Telling It All to Me?" that he was moved to start the Lutheran Encounter Group (Known also as L.E.G. It's slogan was "Get a L.E.G. up on your problems!") at Augustana College.

Unfortunately, the group disbanded after a year, when nobody had been able to think of anything to say. L.E.G. used to meet Monday nights at the Truck Haven Cafe, and some nights the most meaningful conversation was when the waitress took the orders. But even that dropped off when the waitress realized they all ordered the same thing each week, and was able to bring them their dinners just by taking attendance.

Tacit is credited with inventing nonverbal communication. Most Scandinavian/Americans prefer to communicate personal information by osmosis, if at all.

VARSHOGOO
Goddess of Egg Coffee

Scholars can tell us little about Varshogoo that the nutritionists have not already warned us against. One of the chief goddesses of the northerners, Varshogoo is also known as the "Bringer of the Caffeine" and "Pusher of Sugars." During the last month of the year, she reigns supreme, enlisting her devotees in the ritual making of fattiman, krumkaka, lefse, sandbakles, smorkringla, julkaka, saffron bread, spritsar, rice pudding and countless varieties of sugar cookies. Then starting on Dec. 13, Lucia Day, the stored pastries are force-fed to everyone who enters the state of Minnesota.

Varshogoo is the guardian of church bake sales.

TOMTEBODA
Godlet of Sweaters

The two great identifying marks of a true Scandinavian are a love of sweaters and the eating of lutefisk. Both show membership in the great Nordic community—lutefisk by proving what dangers you are willing to endure to retain membership; sweaters by showing that you've got enough sense to come in out of the cold.

The sweater not only bespeaks a generic Scandinavian, but by its pattern, style and buttons, it also tells the discerning viewer where you come from and who your family is. Each valley in Norway has its own pattern of stitches, and families have their own pewter or silver buttons with their marks on them. From my own sweater, an expert could tell that I came from the duty-free shop at the Oslo airport, and that my family buttons show...well, you get the idea generally.

There is a charming myth about how sweaters came to Scandinavia. Tomteboda, the innocent child, came sailing from the west one day on a boat whose sail was a large sweater and whose rigging was made of scarves. She sailed up every fjord, teaching townfolk how to knit so they would have warm clothes for the winter. And for the fall. And spring. And maybe summer too, just in case. This blissful state would probably have continued forever, except that one day the customs people slapped a lien on her boat for unpaid wool taxes.

That story is seldom told anymore, since its moral is sort of depressing, but it remains a charming tale nonetheless. In some of the later versions of this story, Tomteboda grows up and moves to America where she becomes the Goddess of Overheated Houses.

FYDA
Goddess of Compulsive Neatness

One of the oldest cults centers on Fyda, the Goddess of Compulsive Neatness. Archaeologists excavating the bog treasures of Denmark and the ship burials of Norway have confirmed discoveries of ironed underwear and Tupperware. If this is true, the ancient Norse festival of *Husclaenning* would be traceable directly to certain present-day rituals in early spring (long thought to have been a nordic alternative to the fertility rites commonly celebrated in warmer climes).

An ancient prayer chanted by the women of the village reads:

Oh, Great Fyda, help us with this damned ironing;
and cleaning; and dusting; and mopping;
and dirty dishes; and vacuuming; and cleaning drapes;
and washing windows; and cleaning out the attic;
and save us from waxy build-up. O.K.?

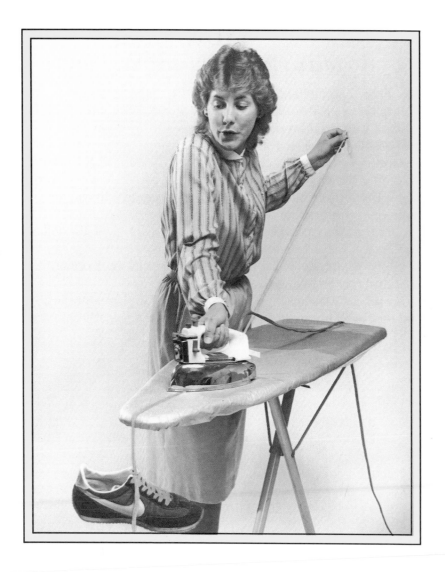

KMUTE
God of Humor

There is substantial doubt whether Kmute (pronounced "Mute") ever existed at all. Some contend that some medieval scholar invented him while transcribing the ancient tales of Nordic cosmology, because he refused to believe that so many people could be so totally lacking in any sort of humor. Other scholars take the opposite viewpoint: Any people who can talk convincingly about the humor in Ingmar Bergman's films have no need of an external power to tell them when to be amused.

Many casual observers fail to notice Scandinavian/American humor because they expect it to have the same level of sophistication achieved by Scandinavian fashion and furniture design. On the contrary, Nordic humor is expressed in a rustic search for new places to put "Uff Da" buttons, stickers or plaques; and in wearing buttons which demand: "Kiss me, I'm 1) Swedish, 2) Norwegian, 3) Danish, 4) Finnish, 5) Icelandic, or 6) Most of the Above."

The town of Vikabu in northern Minnesota has yet to recover fully from Pastor Ivar Hauge's retirement potluck picnic in 1953. Pastor Hauge had ministered to Vikabu for nearly 40 years as a stern, righteous man of God. But when he took off that ruffled collar those old Norwegian Synod ministers used to wear, he walked over to the Oas family's table and not only smiled, but actually told a joke. Recalled Jon Oas, years later: "Of course, nobody had ever seen him smile in those 40 years, so that was a shock in itself, but that joke—it was so funny I almost laughed out loud."

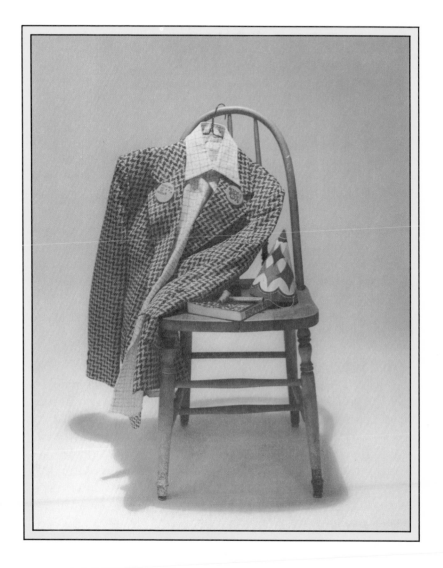

THE MMNSI TEST

The Minnesota Multi-Nordic Scandinavian-ness Inventory.

Scientists have long debated what causes Scandinavian/
American style-behavior. Some held that it was only a genetic quirk: a dominant gene for blonde hair and blue
eyes, and a genetic predisposition for Tuna Hot Dish served on
Melmac.

Other scientists held that it was all learned behavior. *Simple*
learned behavior, of course: simple enough for Scandinavian/
Americans to master.

Some of the latter even held that those behaviors were not
so much *learned* as they were *contagious,* considering how much
everybody else in Minnesota ended up acting like Scandina-
vian/Americans.

The evidence on that count is overwhelming, and certainly
does point to an epidemic. For example: Minnesota's most famous black rock star, Prince, is actually named Prince Roger
Nelson. If Leo Buscaglia had been born here, he would not be
running around hugging people—like Miss Manners—who do
not wish to be hugged. Or, as a recently arrived, non-Nordic
friend remarked: "You cannot remain a Neil Simon character in
an Ingmar Bergman state."

Take a few minutes right now, to assess your inherent or
acquired Nordic abilities. They are the keys to getting along
with your fellow Minnesotans, understanding their inexplicable
behavior and preferences, and anticipating their otherwise
unpredictable reactions.

The MMNSI Test.

(There *are* right and wrong answers. You *will* be judged.)

1. Finish this sentence: "Ya, ..."
   A. sure."
   B. ..., well..."
   C. ..., well, that's hard to say."

2. Lutefisk is to food as _____ is to fun.
   A. A lecture on toxic waste
   B. Solitary confinement
   C. Pain and disfigurement

3. Syttendemai is a celebration of:
   A. Liv Ullmann's birthday.
   B. The day Norway paid off its mortgage to the First Danish National Bank.
   C. The opening of the tourist season.

4. Ole Bull founded:
   A. The St. Paul Stockyards.
   B. The first Bull market.
   C. Oleana Artificial Dairy Products, Inc.

5. "Svenskarnasdag" translates as:
   A. "No Norwegians need apply."
   B. "I thought you said the King was coming this year."
   C. "So that's what they call gymnastics in Sweden."

6. A Scandinavian/American's highest honor is to have:
   A. The King of Norway decorate you.
   B. The King of Sweden flirt with you.
   C. Ingmar Bergman make a movie about you.

7. Old lefse is used for which industrial purpose?
   A. Nontoxic tarps for long-haul grain trucks
   B. Conveyor belts for munitions factories
   C. Emergency tent shelters during blizzards

8. "UFF DA" translates into English as:
   A. "Usch Da"
   B. "Fy Da"
   C. "Oy Veh"

9. If the ELC became the ALC and the Missouri Synod became (in part) the AELC and the Haugians became the Wisconsin Synod,

where did all those Germans come from?

A. The Augustana Synod

B. New Ulm

C. Beats me!

10. When they play the Swedish national anthem at Svenskarnasdag, the appropriate behavior is:

A. Mumble along and glance about to see who knows the words.

B. Sing lustily, carefully pronouncing each word in Swedish.

C. Sing anything in Swedish, and watch the girl gymnasts getting ready to perform.

11. The Swedish Institute is:

A. None of the above.

B. The funkiest formerly private home in Minnesota.

C. Dedicated to research into the effects of aging on group cohesiveness.

12. Carl joined the Sons of Norway to get their special 14 day/15 night *Norwegian Fjord Fiesta*. Unbeknownst to him, his wife Cora had joined the American Swedish Institute for their *Midsommar in Swinging Stockholm* 15 day/14 night Maxi-excursion. When Carl and Cora presented each other with their surprise gifts, it was beyond the 320 day Penalty-free Refund Limit (with 27.5% processing fee and handling charge). What should they do now?

A. Forget it and go to Cancun.

B. Go to Tivoli and get drunk.

C. Divide the APEX Hi-Flyer fare by 1.378, add a value-added tax of .56 per US $10.45, plus a non-landing fee of US $13.74 for each planned stop, convert this fee into Icelandic kroner at the closing currency rate in effect at last Friday's money market in Helsinki, and then stay home and watch travel films on Sunday afternoon at the Swedish Institute.

13. The world's greatest playwright is:

A. Ibsen.

B. Strindberg.

C. Holberg.

14. You have gotten into an argument with a customs official as you are about to board your plane at the Oslo Airport and accidentally called him a Quisling. What do you do now?

A. Nothing. Die like a man.

B. Try to remember quickly which countries still accept hijacked airplanes, and decide if you would like to retire in Syria.

   C. Play the dumb American, and hope to God he didn't hear you.

15. Keyflavik, Iceland's largest airport, can be described as:
    A. The U.S. Navy's favorite R&R spot for personnel stationed in Greenland.
    B. American college students' major potty stop in the 1960s on their way to a cheap European trip.
    C. Gateway to the Vatnajokull Glacier.

16. When milking a cow, the most important thing to watch out for is:
    A. The hooves.
    B. The stuff on the tail.
    C. The bull.

17. Traditionally, Norwegian milkmaids milked goats not from the side as one milks a cow, but bent over, facing the opposite way from the goat, and trapping the goat between their legs. Why?
    A. Oh, they didn't either! That's just one of those things they make wood carvings of, for the tourists.
    B. If they did, it sounds like an excellent reason for immediate automation.
    C. Well, the view may not be so hot, but you can't get kicked, and the horns will give you a nice backscratch.

18. "Snus" is:
    A. A Nap.
    B. On TV at 10 p.m.
    C. Good for you as long as you don't try to spit in the house.

19. Fishing is even more fun than:
    A. Weeding the garden.
    B. Painting the garage.
    C. Mowing the yard.

20. If Lars grows 10 tomatoes a week in his garden from Aug. 1 through Sept. 15, but his family can only eat 7 tomatoes a week; and if Emil can grow 15 tomatoes a week during the same period when his family can only eat 8 tomatoes a week; and if their neighbor, Mrs. Gjemtaas, has a finnicky stomach and can't eat anything acid, how many extra tomatoes will Lars and Emil grow from Aug. 1 to Sept. 15, and who are they going to give them to?
    A. Well, the Stavigs across the street will only take tomatoes if you will take some of their extra zucchini.
    B. But Mr. Oas and that Italian lady friend of his who likes cooking

all that hot stuff ought to take a few.

C. Are you sure you can't use some more? They're great for canning, you know.

21. Why do Scandinavian/Americans raise backyard gardens?
    A. To teach their children, and to remind themselves of the value of patience as exemplified by eternal weeding.
    B. To provide another source of depression by comparing their stunted tomato plants to everybody else's robust and thriving gardens.
    C. To save food money that would be better spent on home missions.

22. Tom Foss mows his yard every Thursday after work except in August when the grass burns. Old Mrs. Gjesdal mows hers every Tuesday morning and uses a power trimmer on Wednesday and Saturday on the tall grass by the fence. Jim and Pat Skjong both have nice jobs downtown, but their lawn is lucky to get mowed every two weeks all summer. Who has the nicest lawn?
    A. Never mind who! What are we going to do about the Skjongs?
    B. Well, I suppose they're busy, but there are a lot of neighborhood kids who would enjoy doing it for some pocket money.
    C. Yes, with two incomes and no children of their own, they sure could afford to pay one of the neighborhood kids to keep it neat.

23. Which sentence shows the proper grammar and usage?
    A. "Well, do you want to come along?"
    B. "Well, do you want to come with?"
    C. "Ska du kommer med?"

24. The main difference between a Swede and a Norwegian is:
    A. Whether their names end in "-sen" or "-son."
    B. "Those other guys are just a bunch of dumb, snus-stained jerks!"
    C. "Well, it goes back a long way, you know, but when the Germans invaded Norway, Sweden didn't lift one finger to help, and they can't deny that!"

25. A Swede is to a Norwegian as:
    A. A cat is to a dog.
    B. Phosphorous is to water.
    C. Salt is to popcorn.

26. Why can't you tell one Scandinavian flag from another?
    A. Because all Scandinavians get along so well together.

B. Because all five flags were designed by the same designer in 1926 as part of a Bauhaus competition.

C. Because the countries have all invaded each other so often that it's hard to tell where one stops and the others begin.

27. Carl's great-grandfather was from Uppland, so Carl will not talk to Waldemar, whose people were from Skåne, because everybody knows how stupid Skåner are. Gus, whose Grandfather came from Värmland, can barely bring himself to talk to Adolph, because those Stockholmers are so stuck up. Who is going to tell them that a Finn just bought the Andrew Fredrickson place just to the west of town?

A. Nobody. Let the damned fools find out for themselves.

B. A Finn? Well, for that kind of news, they'll talk to each other.

C. They'll tell Ethel down at the Sportsman's Cafe in town, and let her tell the others.

28. Despite what some pressure groups say, America was *really* discovered by:

A. Leif Ericsson, known as "the Lucky."

B. Bjarni Herjulfsson.

C. Eyolf the Confused.

29. The most valuable thing my father ever taught me was:

A. How to drive on icy roads.

B. How to manipulate the stock portfolio he set up for me.

C. Never to mess with a tattooed lady.

30. The most valuable thing my mother ever taught me was:

A. Never give Melmac as a wedding present.

B. How to instantly gauge a male's LPIP (Life-time Projected Income Potential).

C. That lutefisk may be served in Minnesota to consenting adults, but is still considered a perversion in many places.

31. The most important date of the year is:

A. The fishing-season opener.

B. The start of crop planting.

C. Our anniversary.

32. Prince Roger Nelson makes his living by:

A. Running a live-bait store in Osakis.

B. Selling insurance for Lutheran Brotherhood, or Sons of Norway, I forget which.

C. Playing loud music, but those kids, they like him, you know.

33. The world's greatest composer is:
    A. Sibelius.
    B. Greig.
    C. Alven.

34. Translate this sentence: "I ♥ NY"
    A. "I Heart En Wye."
    B. "I Love New York."
    C. "You've got to be kidding!"

35. When considering vacation spots, my first criteria is:
    A. Haute-couture shopping.
    B. Serious theatre.
    C. Live bait.

36. The key to fine entertaining is:
    A. A matched set of six rosemaled coffee cups.
    B. Orrefors crystal and Porsgrund china.
    C. Never serving lutefisk in Tupperware because you'll never get the smell out.

37. Finish this sentence: "I recall my Luther League days..."
    A. With delight.
    B. Dimly.
    C. With some embarrassment.

38. "When voting in State and Municipal elections, I almost always vote for the candidate whose name ends in '-son' because":
    A. He/she is obviously the most qualified candidate.
    B. My dad knew his/her father.
    C. I like a candidate who doesn't say much, or make a lot of promises.

39. The last really great movie I saw was:
    A. *The Emigrants.*
    B. *Fanny and Alexander.*
    C. *The Seventh Seal.*

40. My fondest dream would be:
    A. To see the whole world turn Lutheran.
    B. To see the Vikings win the Super Bowl.
    C. To elect a Scandinavian/American President of the U.S.

Scoring Your MMNSI Test:

We're not going to give you all the answers! You've got to figure these things out for yourself. These are all things you should know by now. Work it out on your own—and stop making such a big fuss about it!

Peaceful Coexistence With Scandinavian/ Americans.

Scandinavian/Americans are *very* easy to get along with, as long as you keep your grass mowed and your lawn picked up. And keep your stereo down. Way down. Keep it to yourself, as a matter of fact. Scandinavian/Americans assume that anybody playing a stereo too loudly is probably a drug dealer trying to attract clients.

But we're good neighbors. We aren't always trying to get everybody together for a block meeting to discuss our neighborhood problems. We think the neighbors should already know what the problems are.

Scandinavian/Americans have no problem living among themselves. It's only when outsiders come in and start changing things to suit themselves that there's trouble. These people are full of idle talk like: "Can you tell me *why* you feel that way," or "What led you to make that particular decision?" Nordics consider these empty questions.

I'd like to take a little time to point out a few good things about Scandinavian/Americans, and what a rich cultural diversity exists under the catch-all title of "Scandinavian/American."

I'd even like to offer instruction in the Scandinavian/ American Way. Easy lessons in how to blend into the nation's most homogeneous population. I wouldn't go so far as to say we're exactly *adorable*, but you might learn to enjoy living with us after awhile.

As long as you keep your stereo down, of course.

Shades of Blonde:
How to Tell Scandinavians Apart.

The notion that Scandinavians are indistinguishable from one another is a malicious myth that is easily disproved. Anyone who announces at Syttendemai that he is Swedish will quickly discover how non-interchangeable Scandinavians truly are.

We feel that if the Irish, for example, can distinguish with such clarity and ferocity between the north and south of a single country, people can certainly be expected to notice the differences between five separate nations.

One can easily learn to tell one Scandinavian from another. Scandinavian/Americans make these distinctions all the time, usually with substantial vigor, and occasionally with humor.

To illustrate these vast national differences, I photographed five men from the five Scandinavian countries. Each model is named and his home address is given. Such convincing photographic proof will certainly put an end to the notion of the interchangeable Nordic.

NORWEGIAN

Model: Knut Ståle Bjornhaug
      Smedsrudsveien 28 F
      Tromso, Norge

Norwegians love the out-of-doors and can easily be distinguished by their ruddy complexions, gained from endless hours of skiing. The mountain terrain of Norway makes Norwegians cautious to a fault, and they avoid any precipitate action that might cause them to lose their balance and fall off the side of the fjord.

Norwegians are quite proud of their explorers and sailors. Norwegian expeditions have explored both the North and South poles (neither one is much colder than, say, Mosjøen in the winter), and their sailors have been sailing away from Norway since Viking days. Considering the hardships endured by the Vikings—terrible food, frequent ship sinkings, hostile natives in the host countries—they must have wanted to sail away from Norway *very* badly.

It is perhaps a quibbling debate, best left to scholars, but there don't seem to be many sagas about sailing *back* to Norway.

DANE

Model: Jens Ebbesen
7 St. Kannikestraede
Aalborg, Danemark

The Danes are the most European of the Scandinavians, and certainly the most gregarious. Visiting has always been easier in Denmark than the rest of Scandinavia because Denmark is about as flat as you can get without being bulldozed and paved. This may also explain why they end their names in "-sen" instead of "-son," but I don't know why it would.

Danes are great cooks and hosts. Danish pastries, Danish open-faced sandwiches and Danish aquavit are justly famous. Danish parties are legendary, lasting so late into the night that there is barely time to go home and change clothes before the party resumes with a huge breakfast.

The Danish language looks perfectly normal when written, and can often be understood in that form. But when it is spoken, it sounds like, well, a speech impediment. Nevertheless, Danes all seem to understand each other, and remain cheerful. Perhaps they too, are chuckling about how their language sounds.

FINN

Model: Toivala Maatemelaki
168 Pohjoisesplanadi
Helsinki, Suomi

Finns are the most easily distinguished of all Scandinavians, coming as they do from an entirely separate stock and language group. Finns are known for their high cheekbones and broad faces, and speak an entirely unrelated language, except for those Finns who speak a form of Swedish called Finnska.

Finns are great designers. They have survived as a nation for centuries by designing ways to keep from getting invaded by either Russia or Sweden. After that, designing a little glassware, furniture or fabric is a snap.

With typical Scandinavian modesty (or feelings of inferiority), when the Finns started marketing their dinnerware outside Scandinavia, they named it after other countries—such as Arabia, or Ittala—in hopes that exotic locations would impart a mystique to their efforts. The ploy worked so well that today people all over the world own beautifully designed crystal which they think came from an OPEC country.

SWEDE

Model: Börje Larsson
57 Stora Södergatan
Ystad, Sverige

Swedes are all engineers and sociologists who enjoy pretending they are peasants, even though peasants were outlawed at the turn of the century. The communally minded Swedes were intensely embarrassed at the thought that some of them were poor, so they changed the government, the laws and the rules. That made all the Swedes financially secure, so they brought in "guest workers" from Eastern Europe to do all the nasty work. Don't knock it. It seems to work.

Swedish homes are full of Dala horses and painted wall plaques. These plaques are very attractive, but those decorative phrases on them actually say things like "You have to pay for the second cup of coffee," or "We're going to export socialism to America and make them all ashamed of Vietnam."

Surprisingly, these same plaques sell very well in Scandinavian shops in America, especially to people who do not speak Swedish.

You have to be very careful around anyone who looks like this, particularly one with a calculator built into a painted coffee pot.

ICELANDER

Model: Thorbjörner Sigurjonsson
32 Hafnarstraeti
Reykjavik, Island

Icelanders can be distinguished by sound alone because Icelanders are the only Scandinavians who still speak Old Norse, the language of the Vikings. It is a fact they never let you forget.

They are an intensely literary people, who can (and do) recite page after page of their own poetry, or the poetry of one of Iceland's many skaldic or eddaic poets. They are not impressed with Americans whose idea of literature is *People* Magazine.

Geographical locations in Iceland are often referred to by their literary connections rather than the strict geopolitical notation on the map. "The Gautrek's Saga area" or "the place where Hrafnekel killed So-and-So" are real locations, and can be used as directions. Not by American tourists, of course, but then that's half the fun.

Iceland is the only place where tourists need both a map and a copy of Cliffs Notes for a successful trip.

How to Be Scandinavian/American

Who among this area's non-Scandinavians hasn't thought to themselves at one time or another, "My life sure would be easier if my name were Peterson!"

This weary urge to blend into the most homogeneous mass since cottage cheese has led many a non-Scandinavian on the peroxide path to nowhere. But being a Scandinavian/American is a larger task than simply being blond. Most of us aren't even blond. We just act like we were.

Scandinavian/American-ness is a whole set of actions, attitudes and behaviors that aren't genetic but learned. That's good news for those who want to appear Nordic, for if we can learn these skills, anyone can learn them.

HOW TO ACT LIKE A SCANDINAVIAN/AMERICAN

HOW TO **DRESS:**
　　　　Sensibly. Inexpensively.

HOW TO **EAT:**
　　　　Sensibly. Abundantly. Inexpensively.

HOW TO **RELAX:**
　　　　Read the paper. Go to church. Sleep. Fish.

HOW TO **ENTERTAIN:**
　　　　Follow the menu selection on the back of the Jell-o package.

HOW TO **WARM UP YOUR CAR IN THE WINTER:**
　　　　Start the car.
　　　　Come back into the kitchen.
　　　　Unbutton but do not remove overcoat. Remove one glove.
　　　　Stand over sink, drink one cup of coffee and watch the car.
　　　　Say, "It really didn't want to start this morning."
　　　　Say nothing else.
　　　　Button coat, replace glove and lock the door on the way out.

HOW TO **BUY A CAR:**

Suggest to your friends that you might be considering getting a new car.

Make it clear that you're not really soliciting advice, but accept any offered by nodding your head and saying "uh-huh" as they talk.

Spend the first couple of days checking out Saabs and Volvos because they're so well engineered, of course.

Decide, with regret, to buy a fuel-efficient car instead.

HOW TO **DRINK COFFEE:**

Hold cup with both hands just below your nose, and smell.

Take a small sip and say—with or without an accent, "Ya, this is good coffee!"

When offered a refill, say "Ya, well, just a little..."

HOW TO **EAT LUTEFISK:**

Spray your throat with PAM to help it slide down quicker.-

HOW TO **EAT LEFSE:**

Refuse first three offers.

On fourth offer, say "Well, if it isn't any trouble..."

If lefse isn't already in triangular pieces, tear a triangle off the main sheet. Never cut lefse with a knife. It ruins the bouquet.

Hold lefse in left hand and smear soft butter all over it.

Sprinkle buttered lefse emphatically with sugar—white or brown. (Some people prefer to put honey or jam on their lefse. There is no accounting for *some* people's taste.)

Roll lefse into a tube, starting with the pointy end furthest away from you.

Hold lefse in right hand. Hold left hand under the lefse to catch any sugar falling out of far end.

Eat lefse, making sure to keep lips away from the roll. Do not leave lipstick or saliva marks on lefse. Lefse was meant to be *eaten*, not *licked*. Nothing offends Scandinavian/Americans like saliva, anytime, anywhere.

Making humming and other quasi-orgasmic sounds while eating lefse.

Compliment the baker, even if the lefse is store-bought.

Say that it's too bad you weren't here when the lefse was fresh and hot.

HOW TO **GO TO SVENSKARNASDAG:**

Pick out a T-shirt with something funny printed on it in Swedish.

Wonder whether you should take a picnic lunch.

Decide that it's too much trouble.

Arrive after the program has started and wonder what's going on up there on the platform.

Look for a bench in the shade, then sit wherever you can find open space that's not too close to somebody else.

Watch till you realize you still can't figure out what's going on up there on the platform.

Wander past the gift stands.

Ask your partner, "Well, are you pretty soon done?"

Think about getting a Dairy Queen across the street, but decide the lines are too long.

Buy a Svenskarnasdag button on the way out.

HOW TO **FIX A COMBINE:**

Work at it all afternoon and past supper.

Get your hand pinched in the belt, but don't say anything.

Drop the front section on your foot. Don't say anything.

Go in for supper when your wife gets mad at you.

Mutter under your breath, "All this, and I have to go to Hell too..."

HOW TO **TALK FARM PRICES IF YOU LIVE IN MINNEAPOLIS:**

Don't. Just listen.

HOW TO **FISH:**

Sit motionless in the boat for hours.

Don't mention that your back hurts.

Don't mention the mosquitos that shouldn't be in the middle of the lake.

Don't mention that you're bored to tears.

Say nothing except things like "Who's got the minnow bucket?"

Go home and say, "They weren't biting today."

HOW TO **WATCH FANNY AND ALEXANDER:**

Get all choked up during the Christmas scenes. Tell your friends what bowl/ornament/tree decoration was just like the one your grandparents had.

Hum along with all the Christmas songs.

Tell your friends how pretty the girl playing the mother looks.

Tell your friends that it's hard for you to imagine that the bishop is a bad guy because he's so good-looking.

Come close to losing your composure during the puppet room scene.

See the movie again with different friends so you can tell them the same things.

HOW TO **TRAVEL TO SCANDINAVIA:**

Think about taking a refresher course in Swedish/Norwegian/Danish/Finnish/Icelandic.

Decide instead that it will all come back to you when you get there.

Pack three suitcases of subtropical things. Unpack.

Pack three suitcases of subarctic things. Unpack partially.

Pack three suitcases of elegant clothes. Unpack.

Pack combination suitcases. Lift. Repack.

Forget two things you couldn't travel without. Discover their absence only when you return home.

Bring presents for all known living relatives.

Get hysterical when you land in Scandinavia.

Discover that jet lag is real, but that it can be postponed by hysteria.

Decide that it was the emotional outburst that made you jet-lagged.

Resolve never to have such an emotional display again.

Discover that you should have taken that language refresher course.

Discover that remembering your grandmother's table prayer is no substitute for a conversation.

Take pictures of everything, and from several angles.

Go through your entire allotment of film in the first three days.

Discover that they're really *serious* about eating eels.

Discover that you can flash back to junior-high biology and name every vein and organ in a crayfish, but couldn't possibly eat one because the memory of formaldehyde is still too strong.

Get hysterical when it's time to go back to the States.

Discover that hysteria can be diluted by exhaustion.

Sleep the entire flight back.

HOW TO **TALK MAN-TO-MAN WITH AN UNCLE:**

When you grow to within one foot of your uncles' heights, and are old enough to stop dancing around from one foot to the other all the time, you qualify for Man-to-Man Talks with your uncles.

Go out to the lawn (summer) or barn (winter).

Plant your feet firmly, spread about as wide as your shoulders.

Cross your arms and lean back slightly. (If you are holding something, like a coffee cup, put your free hand in your pocket and hold the cup at about mid-stomach.)

Second option: Put both hands in back pockets, and both of you stare at the ground as if addressing your feet.

Always mirror his posture.

NEVER square off against him so that the planes of your shoulders are parallel. If you must face him, face him at an angle. Most comfortable: Stand *next* to him, facing the same direction.

Stare at the horizon or at your feet while talking, except at the end of a question. Then stare him briefly right in the eye.

Keep it short. He doesn't need to know every detail of your private life.

HOW TO **TALK WOMAN-TO-WOMAN WITH AN AUNT:**

Scandinavian/American women find that the Woman-to-Woman Talks with the aunts come somewhat earlier than the Man-to-Mans with the uncles do for the boys. Generally, girls are considered mature enough to be admitted to serious discussions with the women of the family (excepting discussions of s-e-x, of course) when they are old enough to become the primary dishwasher in their family.

Sit next to your aunt (but not *too* close) at the table of her choice.

Stop the conversation and look at everyone who walks through the room.

Write down every recipe someone else writes down, no matter how awful it sounds. Better to throw away a recipe card than risk ill will.

Ask the aunts to identify people in the family photos. No one will ever resent being asked to retrace the family tree, no matter how often they've explained it before or how often you've forgotten it. It's bound to be more interesting than hearing the uncles retell the same jokes.

Do not ask embarrassing questions when you're looking at family photos. You cannot expect candid answers to questions like, "Wasn't Great-Aunt Christina Gay?," or "Didn't Great-Grandpa Nils have a wife and kids in Norway when he came here and married Great-Grandma Mina?"

HOW TO **GO TO THE CITIES AND SHOP WITH YOUR WIFE AT SOUTHDALE:**

Get up and have your morning coffee. Hold yourself to one cup so you won't have to stop along the way.

Listen to WCCO for weather reports.

Wait till no one is making eye contact with you, then say "Well, we'd better get moving. It's a big drive."

After your wife explains what she's shopping for, let the conversation drop off. Listen to WCCO the rest of the way.

Comment on the same landmarks you mention every time.

Park in the Raccoon lot as always so you won't get lost.

Follow her around while she shops. Stand in the aisle when she goes into the lingerie department.

Hide your relief when she says, "Well, I'm going to be a while. Why don't we just meet at 2 o'clock in front of Dayton's?"

Synchronize watches, and repeat the instructions on time and place seven or eight times.

Walk slowly around the upper level of Southdale, but don't go in any of the shops.

Lean over the rail and watch the people. Wonder if they've just come into town like you, or if they all really live here.

Sit on the benches outside Dayton's for an hour or two.

Talk to other men.

Watch people and wonder what they could possibly do for a living.

Meet your wife. Decide you're hungry but the lines are too long at the restaurants here.

Drive halfway home before stopping at a truckstop for dinner.

Tell everyone, "The shopping was OK, but you could hardly move for all the people."

HOW TO **TELL A JOKE:**

Knot your forehead up and sound like you're describing the National Debt.

Stare at the person as if you're trying to extract a confession.

Tell the punchline. If everybody laughs, smile like you've got gas pains, and look everyone right in the eye.

If no one laughs, pause only briefly before launching into a discussion on the National Debt.

Alternative: If *no* one laughs, laugh like a nincompoop yourself. The shock alone should be enough to make everyone laugh, or at least giggle nervously.

Good and Bad Things About Scandinavian/Americans.

Much has been written about Minnesota's high Quality of Life, but no one has come right out and explained why things are so wonderful here. It's because we're all Scandinavians.

Things around here really aren't all that wonderful, but because we're Scandinavian, we never talk about our problems to outsiders, which makes traveling reporters think they've stumbled onto a wind-chilled Eden.

It's not even true that we're all Scandinavians. There are those unfortunates who are neither Scandinavian nor Lutheran, yet have to put up with us as neighbors.

To maintain their sanity, they occasionally need to make an inventory of our good and bad points, for we *do* have good points.

Here are some of the best and worst things you can say about Scandinavian/Americans:

Good Things About Scandinavian/Americans.

We always mow our lawns.

We know instinctively how to clean fish.

We're really, *really* grateful when spring comes.

We don't interrupt and we always give the impression that we're listening.

We're polite, but not so polite that we seem sarcastic.

We don't generally join secret paramilitary organizations.

Our businesses generally take checks.

We give nearly all musical performances standing ovations.

We generally use Walkmans, rather than VLR's (Very Large Radios).

We don't decorate our homes or restaurants with red flocked contact paper.

We don't view cosmetic surgery as a way of life.

We don't judge men on the number of CC's of internal combustion power they own.

We generally consider pistol fetishes a sexual dysfunction rather than a mark of manhood.

We don't hold loud parties where things get broken as a means of emphasis.

You don't have to speak a foreign language to order in our restaurants.

We don't humiliate people who pronounce the final "t" in "croissant."

Our concept of "sharing" does not include telling strangers the details of our sexual dysfunctions, dependencies and adolescent traumas.

Our ministers do not become famous for starring in weekly TV religious fundraisers.

Our bedsheets are intended for our mattresses. We do not wear them to nighttime gatherings.

We do not grow long sideburns and/or pencil-thin moustaches.

We seldom apply facial make-up thick enough to provide bulletproofing.

We do not use hair spray thick enough to produce a reasonable facsimile of a football helmet.

No Scandinavian/American ever wrote a book defending his role in Watergate.

You don't need time to recuperate—physically or emotionally—from a two-week vacation with us.

We are not barometers of fashion, and thus have escaped Nehru Jackets, Middle-aged Disco and the literary efforts of Gloria Vanderbilt.

We do not consider psycho-babble a second language.

We don't care if we can't tell a brioche from a bagel.

We are not emotionally attracted to snakeskin cowboy boots.

Our women do not wear stiletto-heeled cowboy boots.

We do not give copies of *The Total Woman* as wedding presents.

We do not wear white ties with dark shirts.

We will not blab anything you tell us—whether it was a secret or not.

We do not surrender our cities whenever there is an unexpected one-inch snowfall.

Self-pity is not a political way of life.

Most of us eat lutefisk only once a year.

We are not polite and/or friendly only to those people from whom we want something.

We are not particularly impressed by people with power.

We are not impressed by ostentatious displays of wealth.

Our men button their shirts and do not wear gold necklaces to show off their tans.

It is not a fatal mistake to look someone on the street in the eye.

It is not a fatal mistake for a out-of-stater to drive alone in the countryside after the sun has set.

We are not German, even though they *are* Lutherans.

We do not have debutante balls or cotillions.

Luther League is the most exclusive club most of us ever want to join.

The most meaningful thing in our lives is not our work with our Sorority/Fraternity Alumni Association.

Minneapolis—the Little Apple—is not "The City That Never Sleeps." We sleep regularly, and very well.

Scandinavian/American men do not swagger. It is nearly impossible to imagine them with mirrored sunglasses, riding crops, three-pound wristwatches, or polished combat boots worn in civilian settings.

Bad Things About Scandinavian/Americans.

We make very poor talk-show hosts.

We have cash bars at weddings.

We nod and say "uh-huh" the entire time you're talking.

We give nearly all musical performances standing ovations.

We're healthier, better educated, and live longer than the rest of the nation.

We seldom let you forget that.

We start all our sentences with "Well,..."

We stare right at you when you tell a joke and then don't react at the punch line.

We brag about winters we've endured.

There is no complexion found in healthy adults that is sicker-looking than a Mid-January, Minnesota-Pasty skin tone.

We value live bait more than live theatre when planning our vacations.

Most of our food is listed as a sedative by the FDA.

Because we figure it's *your* job to pay attention and figure things out for yourself, we will, under stress, yell "FIRE!"but you still have to figure out *where* by yourself.

Our idea of an oral history is what we tell the dentist.

We have a nearly pathological need not to be conspicuous in any way.

We remember slights and snubs longer than any known land animal.

We consider fishing an intellectually stimulating exercise.

Worse still, we consider dock fishing an amusing sport.

We carry jumper cables and road salt in our car trunks even in August.

We do everything backwards in church: we stand up to pray and sit down to sing.

Our church music sounds better when performed by a symphony orchestra than when we sing it (or try to).

Scandinavian/American babies look bald until they're about three years old.

We give Melmac as wedding gifts because it's sensible.

We never have costume parties because we can never think of anything to wear.

Ten people, wearing clogs and walking in unison, can make a skyway feel *very* unsafe.

We freak out visitors to Minneapolis by not taking the snow emergency route signs down during the summer.

Which of these pictures is of Norway? Which is of Minnesota? Was it hard telling the difference?

Scandinavian Immigration to America.

The way some of us Scandinavian/Americans idealize our ancestors' homeland, one wonders why we ever left in the first place. The hard fact is that we left because we were starving to death.

Once we got to America and found a little prosperity, we immediately began revising our family trees. Upward mobility can be retroactive in some cases, and we wanted ancestors who were as respectable as we were (or at least as respectable as we felt we had become).

The shame of this is that some wonderful stories about our ancestors have been brutally suppressed—colorful stories about ancestoral scrapes with the law, misunderstandings about paternity, family feuds and other urgent reasons for emigration.

It is hard for people today to understand the emotional trauma of emigration. Our ancestors not only left familiar surroundings and friends but had to surrender their very identities, since a person's name came from their farm or village (Bergen, Herfindahl, etc.), or one's family (Lars' son—or Lars' dottir). Leaving family and homestead meant losing one's identity and continuity with one's past.

There was also the small matter of treason and blasphemy. With the various Scandinavian countries losing upwards of 25 percent of their populations, there were fewer soldiers, taxpayers and congregants. That meant fewer jobs for officers, civil servants and ministers.

Fighting for their jobs, the clergy made it clear that Scandinavians could either go to the United States or to Heaven, but not to both. The military and civil authorities vilified our poor ancestors as well, doubtless by referring to the threat to National Security that these fellow travelers and Minnesota dupes posed to the divinely-inspired family structure of Scandinavia.

But as always, in a battle between bread and doctrine, bread won out, and our ancestors came to a land where they could feed their families. It's still pretty hard to say about that business of getting to Heaven, but it wouldn't be the first time the clergy hadn't waited to get all the facts straight.

At any rate, here we are. Now what are you going to do about all of us?

An "America Letter" from a Former Sailor.

One of the great "Pull" factors in Scandinavian emigration were the so-called "America letters." Emigrants wrote glowing letters home describing their newfound prosperity. Those letters were read after church services by entire congregations, and often contained money or tickets for those who also wanted to come to America.

We have reproduced one such letter below. Written about 1895 from "Sud Dakotah," and written in pidgin English and an archaic Norwegian dialect, its misspellings and bad grammar have been translated into standard English for reading ease. Scholars are uncertain what effect, if any, this particular letter had, but most agree that it was probably responsible for the sudden decrease in emigration from this man's hometown.

Dear Momma and Poppa, and everyone in the family except Onkel Oscar, who still owes me 35 kroner,

Well, it has been a year now since I came to America, and I like it fine. I hope you are still not getting visits from the sheriff and nasty letters from the Bergen Steamship Company about when I left the ship in

Baltimore harbor. Don't believe anything they tell you about that. The captain had been telling me he was going to make me first mate for nine years, and he never did. In fact, they still owe me three month's back wages. At their miserable pay, that would hardly be enough to buy Poppa a couple of buckets of beer.

I like it fine here. My stomach has cleared up and I can eat almost anything, but I still dream that my bed is rocking in the middle of the night. During a rainstorm not so long ago my roof leaked and dripped on my face. I woke up screaming that this worthless tub was going to sink and praying to God not to let me drown with the rest of these miserable wretches. God was good to me and showed me that I was in my new cabin in Dakotah territory, where it is so dry that even the rivers disappear in the summer.

I only wish my screams hadn't awakened Reverend Sommerville. He's a circuit-riding Methodist preacher who was staying at my cabin that night. He said that I said a lot more than I just told you, and he didn't like my tone at all. But I don't think he understands Norwegian too well, so he won't tell Pastor Froiland what I really said. He said my problem was Demon Rum, and the darned fool lectured me all the rest of the night so I couldn't get any more sleep.

This land I own is wonderful! I am in the middle of the entire North American continent, and I am over a month's journey from any ocean! The Red Indians who live here say no one in their memory has ever drowned in water, and they do not understand what it is to be seasick. They laugh when I tell them someone can get sick on water alone, for our businessmen have introduced them to strong ale and aquavit and taught them how civilized people get sick. Just like Onkel Oscar.

I feel so secure to own land of my own, and to be so far from the ocean. I have not been seasick since I left the ship in Baltimore, and the prairie at its dullest is so much more interesting than the sea, which just lies there till it wants to make you seasick again.

I am a very prosperous man here. I have a three-room cabin, 35 acres of land, all of which is flat and can be farmed, and four cows. I am on the committee to build the new church for Pastor Froiland, and will personally be responsible for hauling the lumber back from Minnesota.

If any of you want to come here, I will help by sending money or tickets. Any of you, except Onkel Oscar. You would all love this place, and Momma would be so proud to see how prosperous I have become.

My only sadness is that I have no wife. Carl Oscar—as my brother, will you please go to Synnøve Sigurdsdottir who lives across the valley and ask her if she would want to come to America and be my wife. I will send her a ticket if she will. She should still remember me. Tell her that I was the boy who snuck up from behind and kissed her when she was milking the goat, and who got butted in the shins for my efforts. That should make her laugh, because she sure thought it was funny then.

If she doesn't want to come, or is married, please ask Britta Skjong who lives in town near the butter creamery. Be so honest as to confess that it was you, and not me, who pushed her into the fjord that one Midsommardag. Be sure to tell her that I was the one who pulled her out while you laughed and ran away. Otherwise there is no way she will want to be my wife.

If she doesn't want to come, or doesn't remember me, please ask her who she would recommend among her girlfriends, and write to me with the results. I would like to have a Norwegian wife, and Pastor Froiland has been warning his flock against marrying any of the Swedes from the next town.

I would make a good husband. I am prosperous, hard working, and do not drink too much. I have a good singing voice and am not that bad looking. I have learned to cook a little, but I need to learn how to cook more than Rømmegrøt and porkchops with white gravy. Be sure to tell these girls that I will pay for their ticket. That should help them decide.

Greet everyone in the village. Tell them all how prosperous I am. Tell Pastor Grondahl that I am active in the church here. Tell Schoolmaster Kragness that I still hope he ends his days in the lunatic asylum after what he did to me. Greet all my old schoolmates and tell them how well I am doing.

Write back soon as I am very lonely.

Hälsa Dem Därhemma!

Why Did We Move So Far From the Ocean?

One of the great fallacies of Scandinavian/American emigration is the notion that we all moved to the Upper Midwest because it reminded us of our Nordic homeland. This is a myth so widely accepted that no one even bothers to consider its absurdity.

Compare and contrast, however, the two photos (p. 52). One is of Norway, and one is of the Upper Midwest. Did you have any trouble telling them apart? Did you mutter to yourself, "These two are so similar that I can barely make out the differences!" I didn't think so. Yet every day, we hear someone tell us that we came to Minnesota because it was *just* like Scandinavia.

But what about the weather, they counter. Even if the land doesn't *precisely* resemble Scandinavia, certainly the weather does. It's colder than all-get-out in both places.

The problem with that idea is that Minnesota is a lot colder than most of Scandinavia, which is warmed by the Gulf Stream. Most Scandinavians don't live north of the Arctic Circle. Why would they want to move to a place like Minnesota, which the FBI has described as an "Arctic Cold Front Organization?"

Perhaps one of the most novel emigration theories was put forward at the turn of the century by Professor Einar B. Snakerikke, a moderately well-respected biologist.

Professor Snakerikke spent his later years trying to drum up scientific support for his notion that the mass emigrations of the last century were not caused by obvious factors such as starvation, but rather by a virus which Professor Snakerikke had discovered.

The good professor believed that the virus which caused potato rot was spread by lemmings. Luckily, this highly adaptable virus did not cause Scandinavians to rot, but instead caused them to imitate classical lemming behavior.

Once infected, a Scandinavian would drop his/her worldly possessions and march toward the sea. There they all would have drowned, the professor reasoned, had it not been for the timely intervention of the free enterprise system.

Benevolent sea captains instantly analyzed the viral epidemic sweeping Scandinavia and selflessly guided their boats beneath the cliffs and docks where the stampeding Nordics were attempting to rush into the sea.

When one boat was filled, it would pull away, to be replaced by another. The humanitarian shipping lines thoughtfully took all their charges to America, where medical experts felt that the fresh air and the shock of being dumped in New York City would snap them out of this behavior.

It's an interesting theory, and certainly very flattering to capitalism, but unfortunately, Professor Snakerikke was before his time and never lived to apply for a grant from the Minnesota Association of Commerce and Industry. It certainly is a topic that deserves more attention, and I'm sure that either the Hoover Institute or the Free Enterprise Institute will soon fund further research.

Lutheran Street Gangs in New York City.

It is always assumed that Scandinavians moved to the Midwest simply because the railroads were offering nearly free land, and the climate was similar to what they had left behind.

The real reason, however, is entombed in the sort of silence only rural Scandinavian/Americans can create. We like to call our ancestors "immigrants" and describe their journey as a flight from oppression.

That's partially true: They *were* immigrants, at least until they got to New York. Then, after a short and unhappy experience for all involved, they became exiles and deportees.

This is how it really happened.

Around 1860, the first wave of Scandinavian emigrants fled the potato famines and state-church orthodoxy. They were largely rural people, fed up with sitting around the barn. While they knew there had to be something more interesting to do on Saturday night than to sit around painting folk art on chests designed to be passed on to future generations of antique dealers, they didn't quite know what it could be.

So they left Scandinavia out of boredom. When they got to Ellis Island, they couldn't very well write "Tedium" on their immigration applications as their reason for leaving home. So they said that they were religiously persecuted, which is what everybody between the age of 15 and 22 believes anyway.

It was a grand time to be in New York. The Civil War was over, so there was no danger of getting drafted, and the free (and largely legal) money of the Reconstruction and its attendant speculations was in the air.

Many decided to get in on the speculative markets. Several (17,268 to be exact) even bought the Brooklyn Bridge at one time or another. (The nasty rumor that some of them bought it several times has been proved false.)

This was not because some stereotypical Yankee con-artist got a naive immigrant alone somewhere and fast-talked him or her. In fact, most Scandinavians refused their first offers to buy. Instead, they went home, discussed it with their spouses, called in some friends, debated it for awhile, and then pooled their resources. Some even formed corporations for this purpose.

Most famous of these was the Storabryggagruppen AB, Inc. It consisted of 68 Swedish families (including the entire population of Frilåd, Sweden), 59 Norwegian families, 31 Finnish families who couldn't understand either the Americans or the Swedes but at least felt familiar being pushed around by Swedes, 24 Danish families and a single Icelander, who never forgave them for losing his money.

Based on the German Landverein associations popular about then, the Storabryggagruppen AB, Inc. planned to set up small houses on the upper level of the bridge in an urban utopi-

---

THE DOTTIRS AV DALARNA PRESENT *THE LIVING FLAG.*

The Grand finale of the 14th Annual "Salute to Sverige," held by the Dottirs av Dalarna, Lodge #302, was a "Living Flag" presented by Mrs. Edward "Ed" Nordgren, Mrs. William "Bill" Skogstrand, Mrs. Fredrick "Fred" Nygaard and Mrs. Carl "Carl" Paulson.

The Dottirs av Dalarna was founded in 1958 to help promote understanding between Sweden and the United States. The Dottirs now host a bi- or triennial group tour to Dalarna, depending, and an annual combined Midsommars Fest/Fourth of July Picnic.

Last year, over $40 was raised to expand the Dottirs Lending Library of Swedish travel brochures. This year's goal is set at $75, which will be used to purchase and distribute Swedish travel posters to all public grade schools in southern Minnesota.

overleaf ▶

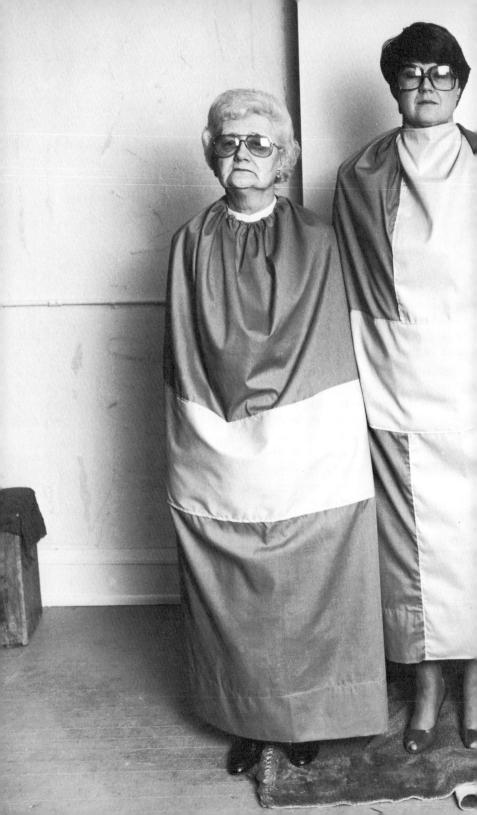

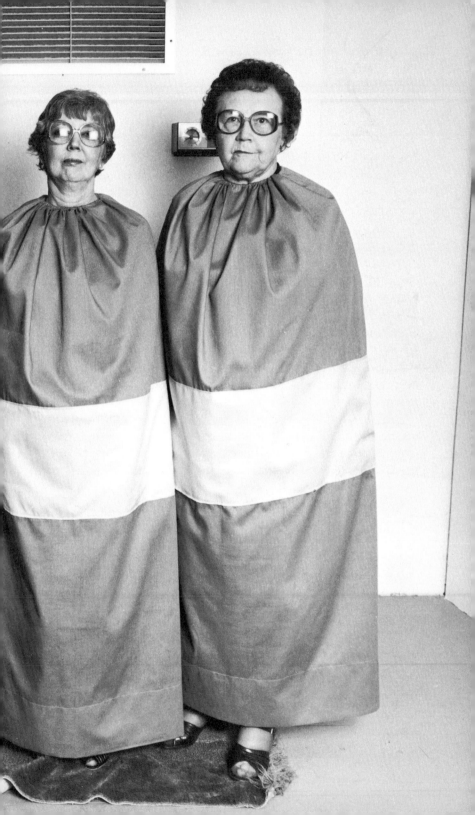

an experimental setting. They also carefully allotted fishing rights to assure the financial stability of the settlement.

Closing date was set for 4 p.m., next Friday. The seller assured them that he would not need to be present, having turned the papers over to his attorneys and bankers.

It was a long, hard week for those Scandinavians, who never dreamed that their new country would make them rich so quickly.

Anxious to begin work on their new homes, at 3 p.m. on Friday they posted signs on the bridge stating their intent to start work in one hour. Unfortunately, the signs were in Swedish, and the Yankees could neither read them nor fathom any reason why they should.

Promptly at 4, in the midst of Friday rush-hour traffic, the Scandinavians wheeled their wagons full of lumber across all lanes of traffic and began unloading the wood. Soon they had created the sort of gridlock New Yorkers a century later were to become familiar with, but which then was a new and infuriating experience.

It didn't take long for a group of enraged Irish cops to arrive on the scene, blowing their whistles and swinging those wicked clubs. The cops were doubly enraged because their own group, the County Kelley Land Speculative Association and Benevolent Society, had purchased this very territory and was set to close on it on Monday at 4 p.m.

They made short work of the new owners, who didn't understand much English, let alone Irish-accented English, but who understood very well those swinging clubs. Unprepared to defend themselves, the Scandinavians broke and fled, running the gamut of angry New Yorkers and their kicking horses.

Now it was the Scandinavians' turn to be outraged. They felt they had been robbed, which they had, but they got the identity of the robbers somewhat turned around. They quickly came to the conclusion that it was the entire New York/Eastern Seaboard Establishment which had done them wrong, so they set out to trash the city of New York.

Hotheaded gangs of Scandinavian youths roamed the

streets chanting, "Salvation through grace alone!" Any police-man with the common sense of a rutabaga hightailed it out of the mob's way.

They smashed windows in fish markets and looted the sup-plies of herring and lutefisk, which they fashioned into stink bombs. A Snus factory was stripped of its pungent powder, and artillery barrages of tobacco juice discolored buildings for miles, giving a new and unpleasant meaning to the term "brownstone apartment."

The turning point of the riot came when the mob set fire to a coffee warehouse. As the thick brown smoke spread across Manhattan, a nasty caffeine high settled over the populace, and things began to turn ugly.

The police, encouraged by the support of their fellow citi-zens, (and only after being promised a hefty pay raise by the mayor) deputized whole blocks of New Yorkers to hunt down the rampaging Scandinavians.

Not only did they succeed in catching the ringleaders and participants of the Bridge Affair, as it came to be known, but their dragnet brought in many law-abiding Scandinavians who just happened to be out for a stroll.

Every Scandinavian caught by the deputized counter-mob was subjected to summary civic courts-martial and exiled to as far as they could be sent. At that time, Minnesota was as far as you could be sent, and in the eyes of some humanitarians, far farther than anyone should be sent.

Whole trainloads of Scandinavians, defiantly singing their rebel anthem of "Kan Du Glemme Gammla Norge?" were shipped off under guard to Fort Ridgely, Minnesota Territory.

When the local Dakotah tribes heard that 300 trains packed with Scandinavians were due on their land, they took it as the fi-nal insult and tried one last, valiant effort to militarily regain their lost territory while the whites were trying to cope with their own problems with the newcomers.

Perhaps unfortunately, their expedition didn't succeed, and Minnesota passed from the People of the Buffalo to the Peo-ple of the Herring.

HIGH-TECH JELL-O: NOT JUST FOR PICNICS ANYMORE!
Would Grandma approve of "Naughty" Jell-O molds and
Nude Jell-O Wrestling?

Blond and Bland Food:

The Delights of Scandinavian/ American Cooking.

Scandinavian/American food is jolly, unpretentious food made by fat little people with raging enthusiasms for big servings. It is not a haughty cuisine full of artistic creations that look like appetizers without toothpicks.

Pretentious food and dining have become one of the major growth industries of the 80s. Scandinavian/Americans should not be considered responsible for this phenomenon in any way.

All Scandinavian/American food pays homage to our ancestoral Arctic homeland. The highest compliment you can pay a Scandinavian/American cook is to say that you nearly went snowblind looking at the food.

Since Scandinavian/Americans consider the use of sharp and dangerous spices nothing but a cheap way of drawing attention to yourself as a cook, our cooks compete with each other to see who can provide the *whitest* food.

Any food which cannot be peeled, blanched or boiled into whiteness is smothered in a Whitening Agent, usually cream of mushroom soup or white sugar frosting.

Like all fine cuisines, Scandinavian/American cooking has a few fundamental rules. Normally, you'd be expected to figure them out for yourself, but I'll share the Culinary Laws of Bengt Olaufsson's Blond & Bland School of Cooking.

Rules for Snowblind Cooking.

1. Pale food is a Preference, not a substitute. We cherish white food because it reminds us of the great glacial ice masses of our ancestors' homeland, and of our own backyards during most of the year.

2. The use of sharp and dangerous spices is nothing but a cheap way of drawing attention to yourself as a cook.

3. Microwave cooking is a godsend to the snowblind cook. It eliminates the unpleasant discolorations caused by conventional ovens.

4. The traditional cook who still prefers to use a conventional oven can avoid unsightly crustings and discolorations by cooking everything at lower temperatures, for longer times than the recipe indicates.

5. Many otherwise fine foods are marred by garish colors but can be made pleasing by peeling (e.g. radishes, cucumbers, apples, potatoes, zucchini, etc.). Never hesitate to improve them in such a manner: No one over the age of three is more interested in the wrapping than the present.

6. While not all foods can be peeled to paleness, they can be pleasantly brightened with any of the items known as Whitening Agents, the most common of which are: cream of mushroom soup, white gravy, Cool Whip, vanilla frosting, and powdered sugar. Use them generously. Your guests will thank you.

7. Never be ashamed of your Pale Preferences in food. The difference between a lobster-pasta salad, and a tuna-macaroni salad is strictly a matter of economic pretension.

8. Never apologize for living in the Lutefisk Ghetto. Every nationality has its own pale and/or bland food, from fettucini Alfredo to wonton soup and Moroccan powdered cookies. Since certain persons believe these dishes are innately possessed of Panache and Flair, it shouldn't be difficult to convince them that Torsk is Exotic.

9. Understand the role of *chic* in cooking. Trendy sorts who would diet before letting a can of Campbell's Cream-of-Mushroom soup pass their lips will wax rhapsodic about *potage creme de champignons.*

10. If all cats are grey after dark, how much more can we expect of food served by candlelight?

Whitening Agents: Even if it can't be peeled, boiled or blanched into whiteness, you can always mask garishly colored foods with a whitening agent.

Campbell's
Cream of Chicken SOUP
Cream of Potato SOUP
Cream of Mushroom SOUP
Cream of Onion SOUP
Creamy Chicken Mushroom SOUP
Cream of Shrimp SOUP
Cream of Celery SOUP
Hunt's Reddi wip
KRAFT 100% Grated Parmesan
THE BREAD SPREAD
Miracle Whip
Pillsbury
Vanilla Frosting Supreme
CLOVER LEAF whipping cream
Tartar sauce
FLAKE COCONUT
NET WT. 14 OZS.
OLD HOME Naturally Cultured GRADE A SOUR CREAM NET WT. 8 OZ.
PHILADELPHIA CREAM CHEESE
KRAFT
C and H
CONFECTIONERS powdered sugar
powdered cane sugar
powdered pure cane

11. Modern science has proved that except for providing a constant source of guilt, food exists exclusively to provide us with warmth and salt. Romance fills the same need, but indigestion is easier to cure than herpes.

12. If an army travels on its stomach, the Lutheran Church ought to go far.

A Small Catechism
of Lutheran Recipes.

Gourmets and Gourmands agree that the finest Scandinavian/American haute cuisine is to be found at Lutheran church suppers.

Even though people often ask for the recipes ("How in the world do you make perfectly good food taste like *that?*" is the way it's usually phrased), most Lutheran hot dishes are produced instinctively, not reproduced slavishly from some dry formula.

On the rare occasion when a recipe is written down, it is little more than a crib sheet—a device to jog the cook's memory. Like all Scandinavian/American communication, these recipes are indirect and implied, and you are expected to figure them out for yourself.

We understand that not everybody has the (life)time necessary to absorb the details of Lutheran cooking. For these people, we have gathered the finest examples of Lutheran cooking ever seen in written form. We'd like to break the Nordic code of silence to share them with you.

Garden Ingenuity
Round and Round with Rhubarb

Rhubarb is a great Scandinavian/American foodstuff.
It doesn't require a lot of fussing, and won't sulk if
you don't talk to it. Its variety of uses are rivaled
only by Tuna and Macaroni in Lutheran Cuisine. Some examples:

Rhubarb sauce
Rhubarb cake
Rhubarb cake with Jell-o
Rhubarb-glazed chees-cake
Rhubarb dessert
Rhubarb-marshmellow cake
Rhubarb dream dessert
Rhubarb upside-down cake
Rhubarb Jell-0 dessert
Rhubarb bars

Rhubarb pie
Rhubarb dumplings
Rhubarb cake a la mode
Spring rhubarb cake
Rhubarb-raison pie
Cherry-rhubarb crunch
Rhubarb wine
Strawberry-rhubarb pie
Rhubarb punch
Rhubarb butter crunch

TUNA TANGO *

— ENOUGH TUNA

— ENOUGH CREAMETTE "SALAD-ETTE" RINGS

— SOME CREAM-OF-MUSHROOM SOUP
— EXTRA MILK, TIL IT'S MOIST ENOUGH

POTATO CHIPS

BOIL MACARONI IN WELL-SALTED WATER FOR
45-60 MIN. STIR EVERYTHING TOGETHER.
CRUMBLE POTATO CHIPS ON TOP. BAKE LONG
ENOUGH. SERVE IN A NICE BOWL.

* THE ULTIMATE IN LUTHERAN CUISINE!!!

Saturday Special

Hamburger
macaroni
Bottle of home canned tomatoes (or Ragu, if you spent
   your summer fooling around instead of canning)
Kidney Beans to stretch recipe depending on number
   of kids
Onions, assuming no one objects
Celery to stretch above
Salt and pepper, onion salt, MSG, Lowrey's, or
   whatever is handy— to taste.
Brown hamburger and onions together in pan.
Boil macaroni till done (Remember, al dente is just
   Italian for not finished.)
mix everything together in pan, or bake in hot
                 enough oven till done
                     serves many children

69

Hot Dish Toppings

A hot dish isn't like Jell-o which can be molded into pretty shapes. A hot dish has to rely on toppings to make it attractive to company and disguise it from the family. While the general rule is that a good topping consists of whatever is handy that crunches, the following have proved themselves consistent favorites.

Chow-mein noodles
Crumbled potato chips
Bread Crumbs
Bacon strips
Baco-Bits

Paprika - lots of paprika
Canned shoestring potatoes
Tater Tots
Crumbled Crackers
Taco Chips
Grated Cheese
Hard-cooked eggs
Cashews and Almonds
(for confirmations)

LUTHER LEAGUE SALAD (SERVES 200)

20 CHICKENS (BROILED, BONED & DICED)
17½ LBS. SHELL MACARONI (PRECOOKED WEIGHT)
20 BOXES FROZEN PEAS
5 BUNCHES OF CELERY   5 CANS OF PIMENTO
10 MEDIUM ONIONS (OPTIONAL)   SALT & PEPPER TO TASTE
5 PINTS HOME-COOKED SWEET PICKLES (CHOPPED, IF DESIRED)
5 CANS JUMBO PITTED BLACK OLIVES, CHOPPED FINE

BOIL MACARONI TILL VERY WELL DONE IN A LARGE POT. FOLLOW LABEL DIRECTIONS FOR STOVE-TOP PREPARATION OF PEAS, OR JUST NUKE THEM IN THE MICROWAVE IF NO ONE IS LOOKING. MIX ALL INGREDIENTS & MOISTEN WITH ENOUGH MIRACLE WHIP. USE YOUR COMMON SENSE & DON'T ADD THE CHICKEN BROTH IF INTENDED FOR SANDWICHES. I MEAN, THIS STUFF IS GOING TO SOAK THROUGH WONDER BREAD FAST ENOUGH & FALL INTO EVERYBODY'S LAP ANYWAY. SANDWICHES WILL REQUIRE ABOUT 25 LOAVES, DIVIDED BETWEEN LIGHT & DARK BREAD. IF NOT INTENDED FOR SANDWICHES, MOISTEN WITH ABOUT 2-3 CUPS CHICKEN BROTH TO MAKE IT VERY JUICY SO IT RUNS ALL OVER THE PLATE & GETS INTO EVERYTHING JUST LIKE JELL-O.

This recipe may not be truly Lutheran since it lists exact measuremen... We can only assume it wa... written down by a coo... who had only recentl... married into a Lutheran famil...

THE WHITE-WATCHERS™ PROGRAM

Many people want to provide all-white food for their families, but are undercut by a world full of chaotic food colors. Their traditional Scandinavian/American food values are trashed by tomato sauce, zapped by zucchini and buffeted by blueberries.

Help is available! The White-Watchers™ Food Program helps you stick to an all-white diet by providing complete menu suggestions—all of them white!

White-Watchers™ understands that even the most motivated persons can become bored with pale food if they eat nothing but cottage cheese and tuna salad. The White-Watchers™ Program printed below allows you to eat a wide variety of foods you never thought of as white! It even offers snooty gourmet meals in case you're trying to impress some Yuppies.

Breakfast, lunch, dinner or special foreign cuisine—it's all-white, and it's all here!

WHITE WATCHERS™ MENU PLANNERS

BREAKFAST
Milk
2 eggs, poached
White grapefruit
Cream of Wheat, Cheerios, or Puffed Rice with sliced bananas
Lightly fried pan potatoes
Untoasted English muffin and uncolored margarine
Pear halves in sauce

LUNCH
Turkey tetrazzini, or egg salad on Taystee Bread
Milk
Fishballs and fisksuppe, or potato (Swede) sausage
Pasta in cheese sauce
Peeled apple slices baked in mozzarella cheese, or bread pudding with
    buttermilk

PICNIC
Chicken salad with Creamette "salad-ette rings"
Green onions and salt (trim the ends, of course)
Creamed herring
Generic potato chips with cream-cheese dip
Glorified rice, or fruit cocktail in lime Jell-O, topped with Reddi-Wip
  and miniature marshmallows
Scalloped potatoes, or potato salad spiked with horseradish
7-Up, Squirt, Perrier, or watered-down lime Kool-Aid

DINNER I "Very Nordic"
Torsk with cream sauce
    or Any fish with plenty of tartar sauce
New potatoes
Lefse with sugar
Swedish pea soup
Rutabagas au gratin
Coffee with cream—lots of cream
Rice pudding
Honey-vanilla ice cream

DINNER II "100% Scandinavian/American"
Sliced turkey and cream-cheese roll-ups
Boiled pork chops with white gravy
    or
Chicken breasts baked in cream-of-mushroom soup
    or
Veal with bearnaise sauce
Mashed potatoes
Baked cauliflower with parmesan cheese
Coffee and cream, as above
Tapioca pudding
Coleslaw
Angel-food cake, with vanilla frosting and coconut crumbles

DINNER III "Kwik n E-Z"
Tuna helper
Jell-O with cottage cheese topping
Instant mashed potatoes
Coffee with Cool Whip

Zucchini wheels and cauliflower bits with Gouda dip
Cream cheese on soda crackers
Apple sauce
Green beans baked in cream-of-mushroom soup
Generic chocolate-chip ice cream with marshmallow sauce

THE YUPPIE POWER DINNER "Daringly Foreign!"
Petite hors d'oeuvre crepes
　　or
Chen-chu-jou-wan (Steamed Rice Pearl Balls)
Potage creme de champignons
Villahermosa (melted cheeses in a mini-boule bread loaf)
Barbados lobster salad
Gratin d'huitres d'Ostende (Belgian oysters and shrimp bathed in
　　cream sauce and sprinkled with cheese)
White wine
Fettucini Alfredo
　　or
Filets de soles bonne femme (filets of sole with mushrooms and wine
　　sauce)
　　or
Coquilles Saint-Jacques a'la Parisienne
T'ang-ts'u-ou-pien (lotus-root salad)
Hun-t'un-t'ang (wonton soup)
Spanish Windtorte (The meringue shell and whipped cream hide the
　　garish colors of the fresh fruit)
Kab el ghzal (Moroccan powdered cookies—"Gazelle Horns")
Caribbean refresco do coco y pina (chilled coconut milk and
　　pineapple drink)

WHITE WATCHERS℠ endorses these *ALL-WHITE* foods from
　　the Jolly Glacial Valley.

WHITENING AGENTS		
Cream-of-mushroom soup	Cool Whip	Coconut crumbles
Cream-of-shrimp soup	Reddi-Wip	Sour cream
Cream-of-asparagus soup	Whipped cream	Cream cheese
Cream-of-potato soup	Meringue	Melted cheese
Cream-of-celery soup	Confectioner's sugar	Tartar sauce
Cream-of-chicken soup	Sugar frosting	Miracle Whip
Cream-of-onion soup	Vanilla frosting	Marshmallows
	Sour-cream frosting	White gravy

CHEESES

Lorraine	White Cheddar	Parmesan	Gouda	Muenster
Mozzarella	Cream	Feta	Edam	Gruyere
Provolone	Farm	Rondele	Romano	Beer Kaese
Swiss	Brock	Brie	Blue	
Monterey Jack	Cottage	Havarti	French Onion	

DESSERTS

Angel food cake
Sour-cream white cake
Marshmallow dessert
Rice pudding
Bread pudding
Vanilla-almond crunch
Popcorn
Snowy-white popcorn balls
Sour-cream pie
Tropical pineapple-meringue pie
Creamy peach pie
Marzipan
Lemon angel-food delight
Mock whipped-cream frosting
Divinity
Mock angel-food cake
Grapefruit Alaska
Snow on the mountain
White fruitcake
White cake
Chiffon cake
Whipped cream frosting
Marshmallow bars
Oatmeal bars
Coconut-macaroon bars
Dairy refrigerator bars
Angel dream cookies
Seafoam nut bars

Unbaked coconut-date balls
Oatmeal cookies
Southern cream cookies
White cookies
Snowball cookies
Rolled sugar cookies
Rolled sugar donut holes
Sugar donuts
Sugar cookies
White sugar cookies
Lefse
Cream-cheese cookies
Oatmeal-candy cookies
Frozen oatmeal cookies
Confetti cookies
Sour-cream cookies
Sour-cream drop cookies
Soft sour-cream date-nut cookies
Oatmeal-filled drop cookies
Apple tapioca a'la mode
Cream puffs
Frozen lemon dessert
Jell-O salad
Lemon crumble
Light lemon dessert
Glorified rice
Peaches
Pear halves in sauce

ICE CREAM & ACCOMPANIMENTS

Vanilla ice cream
French vanilla ice cream
New York vanilla ice cream
Honey vanilla ice cream
Vanilla Swiss almond ice cream
Praline pecan ice cream
Butterscotch ice cream
Generic chocolate chip ice cream
(All generic food tends to be paler
   than whatever it's copying)
Dairy Queen ice milk

Soft-serve yogurt
Banana popsicles
Little, tiny marshmallows
Marshmallow creme topping
Butterscotch topping
Blanched peanuts
Grated coconut
Coconut creme topping
Whipped cream
Cool Whip
Reddi-Wip

PUDDINGS & SUCH

Vanilla	Banana Creme	Lemonade
French Vanilla	Plain Yogurt	Lemon-aid Kool-Aid
Apple sauce	Limeade	
Tapioca	Lime-aid Kool-Aid	

FISH

Perch	Trout	Oysters
Sole	Smelt	Cream herring
Scallops	Sunfish	Plain herring
Halibut	Bullheads	Herring in wine sauce
Haddock	Carp	Herring in mustard sauce
Shrimp	Lobster	Pickled herring
Walleye	Torsk	
Lutefisk	Clams	

GENERAL FOODS

Potatoes	Rutabagas	Fettucini Alfredo
Potato (Swede) sausage	Garlic	Chicken salad
Cabbage	Ginger root	Tuna hot dish
Bok choy	Spearmint gum	Chicken hot dish
Sauerkraut	Corn syrup	Potato casserole
Parsnips	Navy beans	Creamed potatoes
Rice	Great-northern beans	Veal
Rice Amandine	Marshmallows	Mashed potatoes
Rice with cream sauce	Miniature marshmallows	Potato Buds
Creamed corn	Salad-ettes macaroni rings	White gravy
Hominy grits	Elbow macaroni	White pepper
Horseradish sauce	Shell macaroni	Egera
Generic potato chips	Skroodles	

SOUPS

Cream of mushroom	Pea
Cream of chicken	Swedish Pea
Cream of shrimp	Onion
Cream of asparagus	Leek
Cream of potato	Clam chowder
Cream of celery	Potato
Cream of onion	Potato/Leek
Cream	(Enough crumbled soda crackers
Chicken gumbo	will adequately whiten any
Buttermilk	soup)
Wonton	

DAIRY PRODUCTS

Skim Milk	Half and half	Sour cream
1% Milk	Whipping cream	Buttermilk
2% Milk	Heavy whipping cream	Uncolored margarine
Whole Milk	Reddi-Wip	(For purists, and those
Lowfat Milk	Cool Whip	with long memories)

BREAKFAST FOODS

Grapefruit	Cheerios	Taystee Bread
Grapefruit juice	English muffins	Wonder Bread
Puffed rice	Poached eggs	Croissants
Cream of Wheat	Oatmeal	1-Grain Bread™

PERMAFROSTED SALADS

Sour-cream dressing	Onions	Honeydew melon balls
Buttermilk dressing	Radishes	Soda crackers
Blue-cheese dressing	Water chestnuts	Generic croutons
Creamy dressing	Cauliflower	Coleslaw
Cucumber dressing	Chinese cabbage	Cottage cheese
Alfalfa sprouts	Green onions	Mushrooms
Bean sprouts	Bok choy	
Cucumbers	Leeks	

WHITE DRINKS

Squirt	Coco Ribe	Brandy Alexander
7-Up	Pernod	Gin Alexander
Tonic water	Tequila	Eggnog
Club soda	Creamed pina colada	White Russian
Lemon sour	Hereford Cows	Stinger
Sprite	Baileys Irish Creme	Martini
Bubble-Up	Grand Marnier	Tom Collins
Seltzer	Corn whiskey	Gin fizz
Schweppes	Everclear	Coco y pina
Perrier	White rum	Jamaican pineapple fool
Spring water	White wine	
Vodka	Gin	

Surprising, Inventive Jell-O

There's a lot of talk lately about going back to our roots, but let's face it, for today's crop of young parents, our roots are in the 1950's. We have collective memories of vast Melmac bowls of Jell-O at home; fancy bowls of whipped cream-topped Jell-O at church suppers; and melted Jell-O on picnics staining our hotdog bun an unwholesome green.

And though we may have strayed on the paths of Yuppiehood, Jell-O was always there, waiting for us to return. Not just as fodder for our offspring who demand volume and play-value above taste and subtlety in their foods, but for the adults of the house.

Jell-O has gone high-tech. Before your next party, get acquainted with its many entertainment opportunities.

- Use dry Jell-O powder as a topping or a sweetener—on break-fast cereal, ice cream, salads and such! The Jell-O will swell in the diner's tummy, providing that satisfied feeling with less food! It's good for dieting, and great for those "ever-hungry children!"

- Recently divorced people (women especially) who are having trouble shifting gears from "thinking married" to "thinking single," can gradually break back into "The Dating Game" by making "Naughty Jell-O" for a "hot date!" Jell-O molds now come in a broad array of lewd and suggestive shapes for both sexes and nearly all preferences. Order yours from Mrs. Lust, Inc. of Climax, Minnesota!

- If your garden soil is eroding, mix Jell-O into the top layer of soil, and water immediately! You will have a nice solid base that lets air and water seep into your plants'roots while keeping the soil in place!

- If you think Jell-O molds are "boring, boring, boring!" you're probably right! But you can achieve more "personalized" crea-tions with Jell-O at your next dinner party or picnic!

  For the "artistically inclined," Jell-O can be cooled with liq-uid nitrogen (available anywhere fine artificial insemination products are sold) and then sculpted more precisely than tradi-tional Jell-O molds allow. Don't just *envy* those fancy butter sculptures at the State Fair—*make some for your own guests!*

  Less trouble, and almost as "wild," is to sculpt Jell-O using household products! Cool the Jell-O for two hours longer than usual, then, using a *clean* wire in your rotary weed cutter, sculpt your desired shape, using "templates" if necessary! Remember to "keep the wire short," and provide plenty of "splashboards!"

- Your guests will love the novelty of your "Jell-O Placecards" at your next formal dinner! It's E-Z! First cool a 1/4" layer of clear Jell-O in a flat pan, then laminate old "snapshots" of your guests. Lay the laminated photos face-down on the clear Jell-O, and cover with a double recipe of your favorite colored Jell-O. Cut into slices slightly larger than the photos, and place them where you want your guests to sit. You'll have a wonderful time watching them look for their photos! (Avoid embarrassment—don't use rude or vulgar photos, no matter *how* funny they may seem at the time.)

- Use alphabet cookie cutters to cut letters from a thin layer of

Jell-O, and spell out a love note to your "Sweet-ums!" In winter, the letters last indefinitely out-of-doors, and brightly colored Jell-O shows up beautifully against the snow! Just make sure your message is "nice" because it will be around till April for the neighbors to see!

- Everybody but *everybody* adds pineapple and bananas to Jell-O! Stand out as a cook by adding miniature chocolate or butter-scotch chips, chopped olives (green *or* black), niblet corn or tiny bits of cauliflower!

  Mixing chocolate topping with Jell-O just before it has set provides a nice swirl effect! I call it "Jell-O Bundt!"

  Adding pimento bits to green Jello makes a very "Christmasy" Jell-O bowl for holiday entertaining!

- Tired of Jell-O that melts and seeps into everything? Add a packet of straight gelatin and a teaspoon of cornstarch to your Jell-O when you mix it up! *That* Jell-O will stay nice and firm even on a summer picnic!

- For an "Adults-Only" party, add a daring dash of rum or scotch to the Jell-O powder, being careful to reduce the amount of water by an equal amount! Just be sure that this "X-Rated" Jell-O is "all used up" before "The Little Nippers" get up next morning!

- Anxious to "Waste Away in Margueritaville," but got a blender "on the fritz?" Try a "Margueritaville Jell-O Bowl!" Mix lime Jell-O and a little Triple Sec! Remember—you'll have to cool it in the "freezer" section of your refrigerator!

- Everyone talks about "Jell-O Flambé," but everybody also knows it's impractical to sprinkle expensive Cognac over Jell-O (If we could afford to waste Cognac, would we be eating this much Jell-O?). But you can win cooking kudos for your individ-ualized servings of "Jell-O Wellington!"

  First bake some small, tart-sized shells, using either the fancy sour cream pastry recipe from the *New York Times Cook-book*, or just chuck it and roll out some frozen pie crust dough. Keep the center hollow by forming the pastry around a small in-flated balloon. Remember, this balloon will expand in the heat of the oven, so don't over-inflate it at first!

  After baking in a cool oven, cool the pastries, then punc-ture the balloon and remove. Fill the pastries with Jell-O, using a syringe or cake decorator, and cool in the refrigerator with the holes uppermost. It'll be a "sure-fire" hit!

Lutheran recipes
are passed on
through the
generations, often
for no apparent
reason.

The Mystique of Lutefisk.

Every nation has at least one inedible national dish that its people cherish with perverse sentimentality. These alleged foods originated during famines, and were retained to remind young people of their ancestors' hardships.

Thanks to a world-wide improvement in the standard of living, these indigestible ethnic standards are now generally served only on festive occasions, where wine and the good cheer of friends lowers everyone's critical faculties. It takes a lot of peer support—or peer pressure—to force people to eat these things nowadays.

Lutefisk is the penitential food of the Scandinavians. Undoubtedly developed during a period of cruel famine, lutefisk is codfish dried on racks in the icy Nordic air, and then soaked in lye, a major constituent of Drano and old-fashioned, home-made soap.

Preserving lutefisk in lye probably did prevent it from spoiling, although it's hard to tell with lutefisk. While it's understandable that our poor, starving ancestors ate lutefisk to stay alive throughout the long, hungry Nordic winters, it's a cruel mystery why the emigrants brought it with them when they moved to the land of milk and honey.

Our ancestors came to America to escape religious persecution, to escape the draft, and perhaps a few to escape the law. What they should have been trying to escape was lutefisk.

Contrary bunch that those old emigrants were, if the King had said, "you guys got to eat lots of lutefisk!" they would have jumped up, moved to America, and started a *new* Christmas tradition of eating only Bar-B-Qued ribs, or strawberry shortcake, or *something*—just to show that old King a thing or two.

But the Pan-Nordic Lutefisk Lobby realized this dangerous potential for backlash, and rushed to the King. They begged him to lay low for a while—and keep his silver tongue to himself for a change.

With up to half the population of various Scandinavian countries emigrating to America, The PNLL recognized that there were unlimited profits to be made from the bulk export of lutefisk. This was their chance for Mega-Kroner.

The lobby had done their homework well. They were well aware that there were no codfish fleets plying the waters of South Dakota. There were no natural, untapped deposits of lye near Duluth. But the area *was* filling up with emigrants who had endured a couple of Minnesota winters, and were wondering whether they had made a terrible mistake in moving so far from home.

What the emigrants wanted was a reminder of how terrible conditions were back home. They needed to be reminded that no matter how bad the weather got in Minnesota, life was still better here than back in Scandinavia, where they would be forced by dire necessity to eat lutefisk daily.

The Lobby, recognizing opportunity where it lay, set out to stir up a false sense of nostalgia for Lutefisk among the emigrants. Popular songs flooded the steamships bringing the emigrants to America. These songs were secretly commissioned and printed by the steamship companies themselves, who saw the containerized export of bulk lutefisk as the wave of the future, capable of profitably filling their ships after every last Scandinavian had been found and shipped to America.

The songs were openly manipulative and sentimental, and strong men wept when singing favorites like "Kan Du Glemma Gamla Lutefisk" (Can You Forget Your Old Lutefisk?), or "Your Old Mother's Waiting by Her Lutefisk Pot (in Stavanger)."

After the nostalgia for lutefisk started losing its grip, the Lutefisk Lobby began a new campaign stressing the macho aspects of eating something so disagreeable. The macho approach dovetailed nicely with the traditional Lutheran dedication to duty and personal responsibility. Huge posters were spread all over the Seven Corners area of Minneapolis. "LUTEFISK: It's a Rotten Job, but Somebody's Got to Do it for YOUR FAMILY!" was the main theme of the campaign.

Eventually, reality reasserted itself, and the whole campaign just fell apart when the makers of a Tuna Hot Dish mix put up posters depicting a Christmas feast disrupted by nausea after the Lutefisk was passed around.

Now lutefisk is making another comeback. Another generation is proving that those who do not remember history are condemned to re-eat it. We have forgotten our grandfathers' stories of biting into a chunk of unwashed lye during Christmas dinner. We are lulled by the claims of the New Lutefisk Lobby (Neo-Lutefiskians as they are known) that lye is no longer used in the manufacture of lutefisk—caustic soda is the new agent.

The Lutefisk Lobby is counting on an unsuspecting public's unfamiliarity with unlabeled hazardous waste. They believe that we will blindly assume that anything is better than lye. Caustic soda sounds like some sort of sarcastic diet drink, not a dangerous inorganic chemical.

Caustic soda may well be marginally milder than lye, but let's face it—it's still the main ingredient used to unclog drains and toilet bowls. Any chemical required by federal law to carry a Mr. Yuck warning sticker is hardly the basis for culinary delight.

Lutefisk's qualities are hard to describe in mere words. At least in decent words. It's surprising that the word "lutefisk" hasn't become an expletive itself, considering how often one reverts to vulgar and base language to describe the experience of eating it.

Lutefisk has been compared with Jell-O but its texture is more like what I think a jellyfish would feel like as it slithered over my tongue. Its odor lacks the clean sharpness of freshly caught fish, yet somehow it also lacks the definitive bouquet of truly spoiled fish.

My mother used only one special kettle for boiling lutefisk. She bought it cheap at a garage sale, and thus had no qualms about ruining it. She refused to cook anything else in it, claiming that the lutefisk's oil, or aura, or karma, or something, had so permeated the kettle that it was unfit for any other culinary purpose.

When my father, the only voluntary lutefisk eater in the house, died—not too long after eating lutefisk incidentally—my mother converted the kettle into a flower pot. Nothing ever grew in it.

I am not impressed with the argument that consenting adults and minors accompanied by their parents ought to be free to choose to eat lutefisk in private. There is a difference between liberty and license, between freedom and anarchy, and between decent foodstuffs and lutefisk. In proper society, there are limits. And if there aren't, then there ought to be some.

Perhaps what we need are self-help therapy groups, such as Lutefisk Anonymous, for the caustic-soda dependent. Or Lute-Anon, for those of us who are not personally addicted, but who play a codependent role in providing our weaker friends and relatives fresh supplies of this evil stuff.

It's time we stopped thinking of this dangerous substance as a test of our courage, or a public proof of what ordeals we will endure to prove our membership in the Scandinavian/American gang. We need to bring some of our vaunted Nordic rationality to bear on this problem, and rid ourselves of this monkey—or fish—on our backs.

Only then will be able to fulfill the bright future envisioned by Björnstjerne Björnson in his 1896 epic poem, "To a Better Diet."

"And then will come, Blonde Maids and Jarls,
With clear sweet breath, and settled bowels,
Striving Southwards, from Arctic womb,
To share with all, in plain and desert,
A new cuisine, free of Soda,
And free of Lye, which has returned,
To Primal Purpose, a Viking Raider,
On clotted Goosefat, flushing nether pipes,
Unplugging once more, closeted waters,
For all Humankind, its purpose solely,
To scour lead pipes, instead of our colons,
So this be our cry, on Jul and at Easter:
Food for the Stomach, and Lye for the Bowl!"

Avoiding Food That Hurts

We have seen a vast variety of new ethnic restaurants open recently. They are all quite trendy, and the pressures to go to them will be very strong on the Scandinavian/American. I would like to provide a defensive guide to those restaurants whose incendiary foods mean that the Smoking section will be your tongue and throat.

Some culinary background: Humanity has always faced the crucial problem of preserving food. Northern peoples have had a fairly easy time of this. As they followed the retreating glaciers back to their old neighborhoods, they just stashed everything outside the family hut, where it froze solid.

Those who stayed in the warmer climes soon realized that the hotter it got, the faster the food rotted. Even multiple growing seasons couldn't help maintain a steady supply. Luckily, someone discovered that spicing food heavily before it was stored helped (somewhat) to preserve it. And when it didn't preserve it well enough, you hurried and cooked it with even more spices, to mask those little tell-tale tastes and odors.

We Scandinavian/Americans, with our freeze-dried farm goods, have always been deeply suspicious of explosive food. Ever since the Vikings traveled the world, looting and learning about other lifestyles, we have distrusted other people's cooking habits. The famous Viking gourmet, Knut Kneckabrod (who invented Rye Crisp) came back from a raid to the south with a tan, a little gold and a case of heartburn that didn't go away for three months. This research led to Knut's Axiom: The more rapid the rot, the stronger the spice.

Unfortunately, the recent world-wide dispersal of new food technology has not rid us of the old folk technologies of food preservation. Perversely, these old methods have become nostalgically fashionable in our modern restaurants. Nevertheless, food that hurts is simply *not* a cultivated nor cultured concept. One can only hope that these barbaric spicing practices will soon join such anachronisms as blood feuds, bound feet, and head hunting on the historical ashheap.

Restaurants That Specialize in
FOOD THAT HURTS:

Szechwan, or **Sichuan:** These aren't your all-American chow mein/ chop suey/oriental goulash-type restaurants, serving an extremely Americanized version of what could generously be called Cantonese cooking. Sichuan is a province stuck way out in midwest China near Tibet, where life is so dull that they amuse themselves by interfering with commonly accepted dietary standards. If the menu at a Sichuan restaurant says something is hot, believe it. Stick to things like fortune cookies and after-dinner mints.

Mexican: An authentic Mexican restaurant is distinguished by lots of jalapeno peppers in the food and no after-dinner mints at the cash register. If you are with a group that has decided on Mexican food, the best you can hope for is one of those ostensibly Mexican chain restaurants—the kind with blue-eyed, blond waitresses who can't remember the difference between a quesidilla and a tamale.

Italian: Scandinavian/Americans love Italian restaurants because they have the biggest servings of all "foreign" restaurants. And why not? The Red & Dead School of Italian Cooking specializes in piling huge gobs of pasta onto a plate, with just enough pure tomato paste, garlic and hot sausage to give everybody stomach acid.

Luckily for us, northern Italian cooking is in vogue right now, and is spiritually akin to German, Swiss and Viennese cooking. It's a lot of fun, and very gratifying, to go to a restaurant with red flocked contact paper on the walls and demand to be served pasta with cream sauce, or an oyster sauce, or anything Alfredo. You *can* have your bland, and eat it too.

South East Asian: Centuries of invasion have taught the Vietnamese, Cambodian, Hmong, Thai, and other Southeast Asian peoples that the only way to rid themselves of foreigners is to serve them food that is too hot to eat. Some military experts consider this the subtlest form of guerilla warfare. There are lots of little surprises in Southeast Asian cooking, and you may not want to ask for a detailed description of what you're eating.

Indian: Curry is a little trick the Indians played on the English many

years ago which the English haven't gotten around to realizing yet. Still, something should be done to spice up English cooking. All English recipes begin: "Take a pot roast, cook it till it falls apart, and then . . ."

Curry is an extremely hot powder made from a plant that deeply resents being eaten by people. It is this resentment which makes curry so painful. The Indians, who resented the English presence in their own neighborhoods, gave the English *lots* of curry as gifts. If the British ever caught on, they never mentioned it. Stiff upper lip, you know.

African: While it is impossible to generalize about an area as diverse and as large as Africa, suffice it to say that it's hot everywhere. And so is the food. It isn't entirely coincidental that there isn't a single Tuna-processing plant on the entire continent.

A favorite African culinary trick is two-part food. First you take a couple of fingers full of a paste totally devoid of taste. Then you dip that—carefully—into a volcanic sauce. You'd do better to stick to the paste. The sauce is so concentrated that it should be measured out in parts-per-million, and included in some governmental safety program.

FOOD THAT DOESN'T HURT, and Where to Find It:

English: English food is so bland that it is hypo-allergenic and can be used as an emergency first-aid dressing. This is why hospital cafeterias always feature *cuisine anglaise.*

Food is the main method of class control in Britain. The masses are so dispirited by the boring food, and so consumed by their futile search for something interesting to eat, that they have no energy to foment revolution.

French: French Cuisine is longer on pretension than on spices. The French are not trying to get your attention with spicy food. Why would they want your attention? As a matter of fact, they wish you'd just go away. Right now! Go!

Croissants are nothing but Wonder Bread for Yuppies—a bland, squishy white bread that can be easily compressed and desperately needs something else to make it interesting. As the wave of up-scale little French restaurants washes over even the remotest regions of rural Minnesota, Scandinavian/Americans will flock to them for their essential blandness. Provided, of course, that those little cafes learn to serve larger portions.

German: Germans do not tolerate spicy foods because indigestion would prevent them from singing beer songs at the top of their lungs and waving their steins around so as to spill on everyone else. It might even prevent them from making long marches.

Food and beer, mixed in equal portions, are the chief ingredients in *Gemütlicheit*. Spicy food would require more beer, and in many cases, that wouldn't be physically possible.

Swiss: How much blander can you get than Fondue?

Japanese: The Japanese place great importance on the aesthetic aspect of food. This means that they serve little tiny portions so you can admire the porcelain artwork on the plate. Even if the food *were* spicy, there wouldn't be enough there to give a full-grown Swede heartburn.

It's all so artistic and refined that it nearly makes you homesick for a Lutheran church supper, with white styrofoam plates buried under mounds of semi-congealed gravy and lumpy mashed potatoes.

SPICE ABUSE!

How Can You Tell
If Your Children
are
Abusing Spices?

1. Do their eyes water, appear glazed when eating?
2. Do they complain about stinging lips, burning nostrils or painful elimination?
3. Does your canary stop singing when they breathe on it?
4. Do they react listlessly to normal foods like tuna hotdish, croissants or potato salad?
5. Have phrases like "Ay, Caramba!" "Mamma Mia" or what sounds like Chinese crept into their vocabularies?
6. Do they hide supplies of pepper, garlic, jalepeno peppers and curry powder in their dresser drawers or in the garage?
7. Do they make rude remarks during Wonder Bread commercials?
8. Do they skip school hot lunch in favor of taco places and sichuan fast-food joints?
9. Are they no longer able to control their belching and wind-breaking?
10. Is there a thin film of perspiration on their upper lip or forehead?
11. Does their breath reek of Rolaids?

★ If you can honestly answer "No" to six (6) or more of these questions, your child is as normal as could be expected, considering the habits he/she is picking up from you.

Is Lutheranism Genetically Transmitted?

Scientists often ask the question, "How (and why) does someone become a Lutheran? Is it an inherited trait, passed genetically through the generations? Or is it a series of learned behaviors, culturally transmitted?

This is, of course, the old Nature/Nurture debate. On the Nature side, scientists believe that a predisposition toward hot dishes, like a predisposition toward Blond hair and blue eyes, is the result of the inner workings of some Nordic chromosome. They deride the notion of Nurture being capable of producing the myriad of behavioral quirks that define the Lutheran/Nordic lifestyle. "Who ever heard of anything so complex being nurtured on lutefisk?" they sneer.

The Nurturists, however, respond that no random assortment of brainstem activity and DNA encoding could be adequate to teach the complexities, contradictions and catechism lessons that make someone fully Lutheran.

I believe that both elements are necessary. Lutherans are made *and* born. A little blond baby has lots of innate Nordic potential, but he/she must be carefully nurtured through years of Luther League, confirmation and church suppers. The basic material is there, but the character must be set in the Lutheran mold. This may surprise those who think the only molds Lutherans have are Jell-O molds, but the two molds are surprisingly similar.

The whole process may be genetic, but Lutheran parents

seldom trust such intangibles when raising their young. They take every opportunity to reinforce Nordic notions and tendencies. Deep within them lurks the fear that if they relax too much, Scandinavian heritage notwithstanding, their kid will be the first person in the family history to flunk confirmation.

Then all the little Scandinavian flags on the piano, rosemaled plaques everywhere, and Dala horses and straw ornaments at Christmas would have been in vain. They will no longer be invited to family reunions and will be shunned at Svenskarnasdag. All because they put their whole faith in genetic theory.

60 Things to Worry About Before Communion.

The years between confirmation and college are a stressful period when you do little besides worry and argue with your parents.

Despite what parents may think, worrying is the primary participation sport during these years. Everybody worries about being forced by cruel fate to remain a virgin forever. Some kids worry about sports, a few about politics, most worry about grades, and Lutherans worry about communion.

Non-Lutherans may be amazed at this, but ours is a church with few other major sacraments to intrude on daily life. Communion not only provides a handy focus for guilt, but also serves as a source of stagefright for people who do not enjoy appearing in front of a crowd, even if it's their own home congregation. Some are simply uncomfortable about being in front of their own congregation with their backs turned. In some congregations that's a reasonable concern.

As a service to young people who have yet to complete confirmation classes, and thus haven't had an opportunity to develop a full set of concerns about communion, I offer these certified worries from confirmed Lutherans.

1. What if I drop the little wine glass when I'm trying to get it back into those little holes in the tray?

2. What if somebody wrote something gross on the bottom of my shoes?
3. What if my slip is showing?
4. Am I wearing the slip with the lace hem hanging loose?
5. What if I have a hole in my shoe and it shows?
6. What if I have a hole in my shoe *and* my sock and they both show?
7. What if my nylons bag when I stand up?
8. What if I get too much wine and I stumble on the altar stairs on my way back from communion?
9. Should I put Band-Aids on my nipples so they won't show through my white dress?
10. What if I choke on the wine?
11. What if I choke on the wafer?
12. What if my nose starts to run when the minister gives me the wafer, and he gets all grossed out and won't let me ever take communion again?
13. What if I get drunk on the wine, and don't know it because I'm not really used to drinking wine, at least not yet.
14. What if they use a big wine chalice and I spill wine all over my front?
15. Will God count it against me if I take communion when I don't really feel guilty about my sins?
16. What if my suit coat is bunched way up on top of my butt so I look funny kneeling up there?
17. How long should I stay silent after taking communion? Is staying silent too long a tip-off to my parents that I've done something I'm really guilty about?
18. If I sing too loudly right after communion, will people think that I'm not taking communion seriously?
19. How should I look when I'm waiting to go up to the rail?
20. Where should I look? Will an usher smack me if I look from side to side, or up at the ceiling?
21. How should I walk when I go up to the rail? What should I do with my hands?
22. Where should I look when I'm walking back to my seat? Should I smile at, or even acknowledge someone who catches my eye?
23. What if I accidentally bite the minister's fingers when he serves the wafer?
24. What if I stand up or kneel down before everybody else in the row does?

25. What if they run out of space at the altar rail when I go up to kneel down?

26. What if I get an erection and it doesn't go away before I have to walk back to the pew and everyone in the church can see me?

27. What if my trousers are unzipped when I go up, and I don't know it?

28. What if the back of my dress is a little unzipped and I don't know it?

29. What if the minister puts his fingers way down my throat when he gives me the wafer?

30. What if the minister puts his fingers into my mouth and they taste gross and I start to make big gagging sounds?

31. What if the minister shoves the wafer way back in my throat and I throw up all over everything?

32. What if the wafer sticks to the roof of my mouth? When I'm walking back to the pew, will the whole congregation be able to tell what I'm doing if I dig at the wafer with my tongue?

33. What if I don't think, and accidentally stick my finger into my mouth to get the wafer unstuck? Will the whole congregation see and laugh at me?

34. What if the wafer never dissolves, and I have to go through the rest of the service and sing all the songs and greet the minister at the door with the wafer stuck in my mouth? Will everybody be able to tell?

35. What will I do with the wafer when I get home? Could I tell my parents?

36. Why do Lutherans and Catholics hold their hands differently when they take communion?

37. What if someone put poison or acid on the wafer, and the whole congregation dies or starts hallucinating?

38. If the whole congregation dies, who will be around to come to my funeral?

39. What if I get drunk on the wine, and pass out? Will my parents get suspicious and look through all my drawers?

40. Is everybody looking at me when I walk back from the rail? Why don't they just mind their own business?

41. How can the acolytes stand to have everybody looking at them all the time like this? Or are they just show-offs?

42. What if the person in front of me as we're walking back from the rail stops suddenly, and I walk into them?

43. What if someone has stolen my stuff that I left on my pew while I was up front?
44. What if I can't find my seat right away, and have to look around a long time and everybody stops singing to watch me.
45. What if the ushers won't let me take communion because they heard about what happened after the football game?
46. What if the minister just looks at me at the altar for a long time, and then goes on to the next person without saying anything to me or giving me communion? Would I have to join another church?
47. What if this is all a dream and I have to go up there wearing my old pajamas with the rip in the arm, except that everyone in the congregation isn't dreaming and they can see and they start to laugh?
48. What if the minister wants to ask me more catechism questions before he gives me communion?
49. What if the altar rail cushion falls off just before I kneel down and I break my knee and can't get up and have to be carried off by the ushers and everybody laughs?
50. What if I have a big run in my nylons? Will that cute guy from Luther League be grossed out and not ask me out ever? And why is he staring at my legs anyway?
51. Do I look really fat kneeling up there? Are people staring at my butt and being snide?
52. Why did I wear this sleeveless dress? My arms always look heavy and flabby in it, just like Mrs. Strandquist, and she's over thirty!
53. Does that cute guy from Luther League notice how cute I am in this new dress? Is he even here today, or did he go to the early service?
54. Is this dress too tight? Do I look like a tramp? Or fat?
55. Will I throw up if that jerk sitting in front of me picks his nose again?
56. Are the people who go to early service hypocrites because they want to get church out the way quick so they can do something else? Or do they think they're better than we are because they don't get to sleep late on Sunday?
57. What if I sneeze on the bread or the wine and they have to throw it all out, and everybody looks at me real mean?
58. What if someone else sneezed on the bread or the wine earlier and I catch some awful disease from it?
59. Who washes all those little glasses? Are they really clean, or could I get something awful like herpes from them?
60. Will I ever get to heaven living the way I do?

Is Luther League an Aphrodisiac?

Luther League is the triumph of wishful thinking over memory for Lutheran parents. Lutheran parents really believe that Luther League is nothing but good, clean fun, in sharp contrast to the wild depravity of the streets and lovers' lanes that would otherwise lure their innocent children.

The strangest thing about that notion is that all Lutheran parents went through Luther League themselves, and not so long ago that they couldn't remember perfectly well what went on, if only they wanted to. But they most certainly do *not* want to remember that sort of thing.

It is a hard fact of hormones that you cannot put that many young people into one place and not turn it into a hothouse of lust. Not the sort of shopworn lust that adults so love and cherish, but a sort of novice lust—an amateur debauchery for people with very little experience but possessed of vast storehouses of imagination, misinformation and hysterical anticipation.

Deep down in their hearts, Lutheran parents realize that Luther League's true purpose is not to quench lust but to channel it. They realize that sex is a simple matter of imprinting, like ducklings who follow the first moving thing they see. Lutheran parents want their children to be surrounded by lots of other little Lutherans when that magic moment of imprinting comes, instead of out on the streets, where who knows who or what tastes they could pick up.

Let me give you a case history.

Holly Evenson was president of our Luther League when I first joined. She had long straight hair that she ironed and braces that made her whistle ever so slightly when she led devotions; and she wore a one-piece cotton dress which, in all modesty, could have been ever so slightly larger.

I was the star of the new Luther League class, perfect in attendance, and always seated in the front row. Sometimes, I was seated there a good 10 or 15 minutes early if it looked like there was going to be a crowd. And attentive! Lord, how I paid attention to the affairs of the Luther League, and particularly to its representative on Earth, Holly Evenson!

I stood when she led devotions, bowed my head when she told us to, breathed when she breathed, and sometimes stopped breathing when she breathed deeply. I made a commitment right there. If this was what Lutheran women were like, I just had to have one for my wife. If not sooner.

She would stand and whistle out the names of the ushers for the church smorgasbord next month, and I ached to hear her speak my name. And all the time, I stared at her. After all, it would be impolite not to pay attention to the Luther League president. I spent a solid year, crucial to my development, staring at her. Staring, with the intensity only a 13-year-old can muster.

And that was the problem. When I was 13, Holly Evenson was all of 17. Cool, self-possessed, intelligent and 17. With an 18-year-old boyfriend—the vice-president of Luther League and center on the school basketball team.

When he stood in front of her table to lead us in songs, she stared hard at his back (she was what we would now call "A buns woman"). Sometimes during these stares, our eyes would meet by accident, and I always took her embarrassment as some sort of secret sign. Unfortunately, at 13, I wasn't sure what any of the signs meant.

But I knew that Holly wasn't going to wait for me. She was going to St. Olaf next year, and couldn't even remember my name when I tried to talk to her after Luther League, so I didn't have much hope. I never did tell her what a crush I had on her. I figured that if she didn't smack me, she'd have sent her boyfriend after me. Either way, I would have had my heart broken, and he would likely have broken a whole lot more.

But Luther League had accomplished its task. Like a horny little duckling, I was forever imprinted on Lutheran women. I had classmates who spent those formative years fiddling around with cars, or playing sports. They're married now, to women, of course, but the spark isn't always there. Their wives sense it, but there isn't much they can do about it. They try to rekindle that old flame by using perfumes that smell like transmission fluid or sweatsocks, but the effect is only transitory. But all my wife has to do is to wave a hymnal my way and we don't answer the phone all day.

I wonder if it's true that Holly married a Lutheran minister?

30 Reasons Why Your Mother Told You To Never Marry a Non-Scandinavian.

Children can go bad in many ways. They can besmirch the family name by joining a terrorist organization, turning their Boy Scout troop into a base for smuggling cocaine, or defrauding the widows and orphans of martyred missionaries of their pensions.

While no Scandinavian/American parent would wish such a fate for their child, there is a fate that's even worse. The kid could marry a non-Scandinavian. What Tension! An entire lifetime of tight-lipped family gatherings just because your child married someone whose name ended in a vowel instead of "-son."

Luther League was invented for the very purpose of exposing horny nordic teenagers to fellow Scandinavian/Americans, letting them imprint on blue-eyed blondes like ducklings following the first moving thing.

Nevertheless, Scandinavian/American mothers are careful not to leave anything to chance. Alternately frightening their offspring and bribing them, they drive home ideas like these.

You shouldn't marry a non-Scandinavian because:

1. None of your kids will be blond.
2. Who knows what church they'll go to?
3. You have no idea how they carry on at some churches!
4. Your spouse won't know how to make lefse or lutefisk.
5. Your in-laws will make fun of you because you eat lutefisk.
6. You'll get indigestion from their spicy food.
7. Your spouse will make you spend every holiday with their family.
8. Your new in-laws will be loud and argumentative. Reunions could be outright dangerous.
9. You'll be marrying into a family that talks just to hear themselves talk.
10. No matter what nationality your intended might be, you'll be marrying beneath you.

11. Your wife probably won't even know how to make bread. She'll just want to spend your money at the bakery instead of doing a little work.
12. Passionate men may seem real attractive at your age, but do you want your kids growing up around that kind of an example?
13. Your kids won't even have blue eyes!
14. Your spouse will make you move out of the Midwest, because there aren't many of *them* living here. Then how often will you be able to get home to visit?
15. You won't be able to help your kids through confirmation, because other churches don't use Luther's Small Catechism.
16. You won't be able to get a word in edgewise with that group because they're so pushy.
17. At Thanksgiving, they stuff the turkey with pasta! Did you know that?
18. Those people will try anything that pops into their head, just for the sake of something new! There's no stability in a life like that.
19. People who live in big houses like that in town have no money in the bank, but they think they're better than everyone else. It's better to have land of your own.
20. Your wife won't know how to knit sweaters. Even if she does, it will probably be some thin little thing just for show, and it won't keep you warm.
21. Your wife will spend all your money on makeup and jewelry, and you'll have to work overtime to buy school notebooks for your kids. And who knows how many she'll make you have?
22. Your husband will lie around all day and expect you to support him.
23. The only thing worse than a lazy husband is a know-it-all who thinks he's smarter than any woman.
24. Any man who is as vain as he is already will be big trouble when he hits his Mid-Life Crisis. He'll either dump you for a bimbo or have endless affairs. His type is famous for that sort of thing.

25. Nobody else celebrates Lucia Day. They don't even celebrate Christmas in the same way!
26. Your spouse and In-Laws will make fun of you and say you have an accent just because you don't talk like them.
27. Other churches don't have a nice youth group like Luther League. It seems like you're always reading about one of their kids getting into some sort of trouble.
28. Your spouse will be a spendthrift. Being charming doesn't count for much when you don't have any more money.
29. Not everybody has the same moral standards as we do, you know.
30. Because they're not Lutheran!

Lutheran Church Suppers:
The Mother of Manners

The average Scandinavian/American develops most of his/her social skills at church suppers in the basements of various Lutheran churches. It's doubtful whether Emily Post, Miss Manners, or any of the other social arbiters of our economic betters have ever eaten a meal in a Lutheran church basement.

Nevertheless, I believe that they would approve of the very pragmatic form of etiquette taught there. While it is certainly not ostentatious (More than one plastic fork per paper plate would be just plain foolishness), it does teach the basic rule of etiquette: Common sense respect for the rights of others.

Lutheran church suppers teach skills that remain useful as long as you live: The correct manner of holding a paper plate to prevent it from folding and dumping everything into your lap; the importance of not piling up your plate like there was no tomorrow ('Save some of that hot dish for the rest of us in line, OK?'); and the topics of conversation to avoid (pointing out that the Scandinavian countries are functionally socialist will *not* get you invited back).

Here then are the basic social skills which Scandinavian/Americans learn before confirmation, the Nordic equivalent to a debutante ball.

General Skills Learned at Church Suppers:

1. How to balance a flimsy paper plate on one knee and Kool-Aid on the other.
2. How to load up your plate with potatoes and buns to conceal the lack of lutefisk.
3. How to manage the Fork/Spoon Flash—a two-handed sleight of hand (or stomach) where a small forkful of lutefisk is instantaneously followed by heaping spoonfuls of potatoes.
4. How to smile and carry on a coherent conversation while eating lutefisk.
5. How to choose the best seat at a long table so as to avoid bores, fanatics and spitters.
6. How to entertain yourself (as a child, teenager or single adult) without drawing the attention or disapproval of your elders.
7. How to laugh with your mouth full, neither choking nor dislodging.
8. How to avoid paranoia when no one at the table says anything throughout the meal.

Tactical Skills Learned at Church Suppers:

1. It is easier to go back for seconds than to overload a paper plate.
2. Avoid Jell-O, fruit salads and watery hot dishes when loading a paper plate. All Lutheran churches buy their paper plates in bulk from a company known as Lutho-Poof, a manufacturer of squirting carnations and whoopee cushions. The plates are rigorously engineered to dissolve in half the time a communion wafer does. A mere tablespoon of warm Jell-O will quickly eat the bottom out of your plate, or cause the whole plate to bend at your thumb within 2.75 feet of your seat.
3. Always hold paper plates with both hands. While this means you will have to go back for your Kool-Aid, it does prevent the plate from folding.
4. Never hold your paper plate with the palm of your hand. Not all hot dishes are appropriately lukewarm, especially the ones in little wicker diapers. Remember also, that anything with a little candle underneath can give you second-degree burns right through a paper plate. Better to have the bottom give out onto the church basement floor.
5. Coffee drinking is the only positively reinforced behavior at Lu-

theran church suppers. Someone will always come around to refill your coffee cup, but you will have to get up and fetch your own milk or kool-aid.

6. Never salt anything before you taste it, no matter how bland it looks. The cook will be sitting next to you, and it will take years of good behavior to wash away that insult to her cooking skills.

Philosophical Skills Learned at Church Suppers:

1. It is neither wise nor discreet to discuss matters of great tension at Lutheran church suppers. These subjects include, but are not limited to:
The failure of the capitalistic system.
The shocking sex practices of your peers.
The disgusting sex-lives of your elders.
Martin Luther's preoccupation with his bowel movements.
The difficulties of potty training a baby.
Cute ways your baby (baby sister/brother) has described its genitals.
Your new job as a lab technician at the local VD clinic.
The details of your dairy herd's artificial insemination program.
Growth patterns of Botulism toxins in uncovered, unheated Food.
Communicable diseases which can be spread by a common serving spoon.

2. The hot dish with the greatest percentage of noodles is the least likely to have an 'innovative' taste.

3. Teenagers are expected to display better manners at church suppers than at high school hot lunch because there are no disruptive outside influences.

4. Digging through a hot dish to avoid objectionable foodstuffs i.e. olives, onions, mushrooms, etc.) while people are standing in line behind you is frowned upon.

5. Expressing a novel opinion on the taste of a hot dish is never safe. Your church is not that big, and the cook, or her relatives and friends are always within earshot.

6. Scandinavian/Americans have food fights only when more than four cooks bring the Tuna-Con-Carne-Casserole as featured in last month's *Woman's Day* magazine, and even then, it's more of a food sulk than a real food fight.

Are State High School Basketball Tournaments Only Orgies With Training Wheels?

As a good Lutheran boy growing up on the frozen Lutheran prairies of Minnesota, I learned with some envy of the thrills and excesses of Mardi Gras and Carnival. To be honest, at the time I was quite shocked. But then I was also quite shocked by the carryings-on of my classmates at the Minnesota State Basketball Tournament. It never occurred to me that the state basketball tournament was only a Lutheran version of Mardi Gras.

Granted, Mardi Gras comes earlier in the calendar year, representing a last fling before the denial of Lent. The basketball tournament, on the other hand, represents a fling after the denial of a Minnesota winter. Both are characterized by behavior heartily condemned by nonparticipants and considered wholly therapeutic by the celebrants. Both have orgiastic overtones and, like Halloween, both offer people a chance to assume another identity.

Sports were never the all-consuming passion in my high school that they seemed to be in other schools. This had only one drawback: Even though we were the biggest town around, we never got past the district playoffs in basketball.

At that point, my already marginal interest came to a screeching halt. It was hard enough for me to work up an enthusiasm when my own classmates were out there sweating and puffing. It was impossible to feign interest in watching total strangers (Who were, by definition, better basketball players than we were) run onto the floor and pat each other's fannies.

Already you can see my naivete: I thought that going to a basketball tournament meant having to go to basketball games.

It always baffled me that even though our team was eliminated early in the playoffs, there were 20 or 30 kids every year who couldn't wait to get to the Twin Cities for the tournament. Some were cheerleaders and athletes with a professional interest in the proceedings. But most were student-government types—straight kids who got along well with adults, and were therefore vaguely suspect to the rest of us.

There were even a number of Luther League officers in this annual Tournament trip, MeloDee Larson in particular. MeloDee was the kind of teenager whom adults pointed to as a good example for the rest of us.

MeloDee came from a good family, sang in three choirs and was an officer in Luther League, student government and the Young Republicans. She was attractive, somewhat conservatively tailored, and bright.

I received a significant portion of my education from MeloDee one lunch hour when I was in eighth grade, and MeloDee was in eleventh. MeloDee had recently returned from the state basketball tournament, and was filling in two of her girlfriends on the details. It seems that MeloDee and 10 other kids from our school had taken a room in a fancy hotel that was entirely filled with other high-school students attending the basketball tournament.

MeloDee spun a tale of debauchery, beer and sexual abandon to her girlfriends as they sat around her in the band room. I happened to overhear her wonderful tale because I was seated on a tuba case in the instrument-storage room. I had gone there to get my coronet, but when they came into the band room, I couldn't very well just barge in on them. It was awfully dark in there, but I stayed anyway, hoping desperately that they would keep talking, wishing that MeloDee would speak up, and praying that they wouldn't come into the storage room for their clarinets.

Inflamed as I was by MeloDee's tale of the Twin Cities, it probably seems strange that I never attended a state basketball tournament while I was in high school. The idea, however, stayed with me as a major erotic fantasy. Let the effete and over-cultured have their pale fantasies of French maids named Fifi—I want me a screaming cheerleader with her face painted in school colors!

My high-school class is about to have its 20th reunion. I've been carrying around this increasingly frayed tournament

Are State Basketball Tournaments only orgies with training wheels? There are 7,000 people here, 15,000 seats, and 23,000 kids in the Twin Cities, all swearing that they were at the game...

fantasy all these years, so I finally decided to act on the impulse. This year—for the first time—I went to a state high school basketball tournament.

I knew I probably shouldn't have, but the demands of honest research for this book compelled me. I *had* to see whether things were as lusty as MeloDee's story and my memory had made them out.

Nothing deflates a man's fantasies about high school as thoroughly as having a high-school cheerleader call him "Sir."

The state basketball tournament game I attended was far more sedate than I had expected. There was none of the towering Wagnerian *angst* about winning and losing that I remembered from my high-school days. A smattering of students had painted their faces in school colors, but even that seemed more rational and deliberative than primal and abandoned.

Just as I was ready to dismiss the whole process, I felt something powerful and atavistic rise within me. You cannot sit among thousands of cheering, chanting people, frenzied by brass bands and large drums, and remain dispassionate. A crowd doesn't cheer as much as it throbs. A large auditorium can suddenly seem like an awfully small place when it's filled with all that sound and sweat.

Combine that narcotic noise with all those wonderful quasi-naked bodies—cheerleaders, players, dance lines and some fans—with the brass and the drums, and you've got a perfect formula for a fertility rite.

I noted with vulgar satisfaction that of the 15,000 seats in the auditorium, 6,000 were empty. I also knew that there were 23,000 people in St. Paul that weekend, every one of whom would swear to have been at the tournament. By my count, that's 14,000 kids who had temporarily escaped adult scrutiny and supervision.

Since the game was remarkably one-sided, I went to talk with some of today's typical youth. What I found were three well- scrubbed basketball players from Fairmont.

Their team·hadn't made it beyond playoffs (I felt an immediate bond) but they had come to the Cities for the tournament.

"Oh, really," I oozed, "tell me about that."

They openly admitted to coming to the tournament every year to get wild and crazy. (I knew it! MeloDee was right!) But their rebellion was so sedate! Their wild and crazy only meant a little beer, a chance to be loud and dumb on the city streets, and some whistling at the girls in town for the tournament.

As they explained their idea of a weekend of liberation, I began to feel, for the very first time, a sense of pity for the jocks and the proper kids of the world.

It's been said that student athletes are the only teenagers that adults give a damn about. They certainly are the teenagers who are under the closest adult scrutiny. "Wild" kids get a lot of attention from adults too, but they've got nothing further to lose if they misbehave. A high-school hero has a long way to fall in a small town, and it doesn't take much provocation for the adults to give him a little push.

So they cherish their chance to come to the big city and be anonymous—to be teenage nincompoops, instead of proper little Junior Civic Ambassadors.

It seems to me like a pitiful rebellion, but since I am neither their parents nor a member of an athletic booster club, I am not in a position to be shocked by their trip to the Big City.

Now I don't honestly know what to think of MeloDee's story. She may even have been telling the truth, but that would mean that either my high school was an asylum for sex maniacs (and I certainly missed that), or today's youth has done a sharp turnabout, rejecting sensual pleasures for the Higher Things adults are continually preaching about. Somehow, neither alternative seems very likely.

All I know is that I've lost one of my favorite fantasies.

Schooling For Scandinavian/Americans:

*The Importance of a G*L*C.*

S candinavian/Americans put great emphasis on schooling for their children. Every Scandinavian/American parent wants their child to go to a *good* college. A *good* college according to most Scandinavian/American parents, is one where there is:

1) A great choir or band, *and*
2) Semi-mandatory Lutheran chapel.

In other words, a Good *Lutheran* College (G*L*C).

Failing this, most Scandinavian/American parents have to settle for any old (non-Lutheran) school like Harvard, Yale, Oxford or whatever.

Scandinavian/American young people, on the other hand, choose a college (when they use any deliberative process at all) on the basis of important things like the male/female ratio, and the number and intensity of bawdy stories from older friends about a particular college. This process seldom leads directly to a Lutheran college, but between this and the pressure from their parents, they often compromise on a G*L*C.

How to Choose a Lutheran College
Traditional Method #1.

25 Reasons To Go To a Good Lutheran College.

One day when you are in 11th grade, your school counselor pulls you out of study hall, plunks you down in his tiny office and demands that you plan your life in the next half hour.

And there you sit, surrounded by college catalogues from colleges you can't begin to afford, universities that wouldn't take someone with your grades on a dare, junior colleges that train you to be a McDonald's manager, and vocational schools that at least don't require Phy.Ed.

And the Army. The nicest brochures in the room are from the Army. Only Sun Myung Moon's brochures have glossier pictures of well-scrubbed, smiling, wholesome-looking people than the Army brochures. Unfortunately, neither organization mentions their pay scales or their working conditions.

Naturally, you start grabbing at straws. You grab the first college catalogue with the word "Lutheran" on it and send in the response card. Next thing you know, you've just completed four years of studying the transcripts of the Diet of Worms, and you're on your way to the seminary for another couple of years of intensive catechism.

That's not a very positive way to approach the Lutheran college system. I myself am a product of Lutheran higher education, and during my four years on campus I often asked myself why I was there. All my friends did. In fact, it's safe to say that we spent all four years agonizing over why we were there.

We'd like to share the fruits of our deliberations with you. If you are a high school student now, this will surely help you decide to go to a good Lutheran college. If you have already gone to a good Lutheran college, it will refresh your memory about why you went there.

1. Your parents think it is a good idea and will pay for it.
2. Your parents want you to go there to get away from those bad influences (i.e: Non-Scandinavians) you've been hanging out with.
3. Your parents thought it was a good idea, and you didn't have any

opinions about it one way or the other.

4. All your friends from Luther League are going there.
5. You want to become a Lutheran minister.
6. You figure it will be easier than the university.
7. It's more than 150 miles from home.
8. You really enjoyed high school football, but nobody else recruited you.
9. You're very good at music and your highest ambition is to be the Music Director at Mount Olivet Lutheran Church.
10. You want to play basketball, but this was the best package and bonus money anybody offered you.
11. You're too smart to believe all the scare talk about secular-humanists, but you'd really rather go to a college in a small town.
12. You believe the scare talk about secular-humanists and figure it's your Christian duty to straighten out all those atheistic religion professors.
13. You believe that a degree in religious anthropology will help you better serve humanity.
14. You want to go to a college that will give you class credit for learning Norwegian/Swedish/Danish/Finnish/Icelandic/All of the Above.
15. You relish the idea of going to a college that offers classes in New Testament Greek so you can translate Luther League terms like kerygma, agape, and eschatology.
16. There are buildings on campus bearing your family's name, and all your relatives have gone there since it was a prairie normal school.
17. If you had *wanted* to go to a fundamentalist college, you would have said so. In tongues.
18. The college actually offered you a scholarship for your scholarship.
19. You are a PK. While everybody expects a PK to act a little crazy, they also expect you to go to a Lutheran college and get yourself straightened out.
20. You won a scholarship in the Luther League Essay Contest by writing on "Salvation Through Grace Alone In The Modern World."
21. Ever since you got too old to be an acolyte, you feel your religious life has been lacking something. You now see that a Lutheran college can fill that void with daily chapel services.
22. It's a good way to prepare for the Peace Corps.
23. It's a good way to prepare to be a military officer.

24. You feel that nursing is not only a selfless, sharing, caring profession, but a truly glamorous way of life, just like on "General Hospital."
25. You believe what your mother told you about teaching being a respected and secure line of work.

"Where do They Find These People?"
A Field Guide to Lutheran College Types

Despite their tranquil appearances, Lutheran colleges often have a number of characters who are rowing with only one oarlock. And like Luther League, Lutheran colleges are full of people who will come back to haunt you later in life.

THE FEMALE EXILE. A woman sent by her parents to a remote Lutheran college to remove her from her unacceptable (i.e., non-Scandinavian) boyfriend. Often wrongly considered a variation of THE BRIDE (see below). The Exile, however, having tasted of the Neon Nights, may breed in captivity but definitely does not mate.

THE MALE EXILE. A man sent by his parents to an isolated Lutheran college to "settle down," i.e., stop drinking and/or smoking pot. Occasionally, Male and Female Exiles will find each other in their banishment, and the resulting collision (and collusion) becomes the subject of gossip for endless reunions to come.

Both Male and Female Exiles inevitably return home after graduation, open a Lutheran Brotherhood Insurance Agency, take winter vacations in mildly exotic locations (haven't you ever wondered what sort of person goes to Club Med?) and eventually exile their children to a prairie Lutheran college. Lutherans love tradition.

THE BRIDE, or THE SEARCHER. A type amazingly unchanged by the women's revolution of the past 20 years. Her favorite TV show is still "Diamonds for Dollies." Her biological clock-radio is set to go off at 21 with a loud wake-up version of the Wedding March. Young men who do not yearn for the instant respectability of family, mortgage and multiple fatherhood would do well to find dates at N.O.W. rallies.

THE PRE-SEM. Lutheran colleges hold a rude awakening for those who feel themselves called by God to the Lutheran ministry, for first they will find themselves called by the college to classes in New Testament Greek. Because Pre-Sems take on the personality of their colleges and times like chameleons, their personalities range from hip to hellfire.

THE PK. Lutheran colleges serve as an elaborate form of house arrest for errant younger members of the Lutheran theocracy. Theatrical excesses and splashy rebellions against the father/pastor figure can work their way through the pastor's kid's system at a comfortable remove from the scrutiny of the whole congregation, while never actually leaving the familiar structure of Lutheran discipline. PK's are as unpredictable in later life as they have been throughout their youth, and can be found in nearly any shocking occupation, from "exotic" dancer to the Lutheran ministry.

SINCERITY CENTRAL. An innocent, credulous sort who approaches life swaddled in sincerity but unaided by either original thinking or any comprehension of the world about him/her. Generally from financially secure families, he/she often chooses a career like counseling, practicing a gentle but ineffective therapy which is usually called "Holistic" something-or-other.

THE TRUTH TELLER. The obverse of Sincerity Central, he/she loves to "make people face up to the facts," or "confront people with their need for forgiveness," preferably with lurid details of their private lives. Passionately attached to any truth that hurts someone else, the Truth Teller frequently leads a secret life of unspeakable tackiness which is later exposed in the most amusing scandal his/her town has seen in years.

THE SACRED-WRITINGS MAJOR. Noted for an ability to discover theological implications in *any* assigned text, he/she generally does very well in religion classes, but requires *extremely* sympathetic and understanding professors in English, art, economics and political science. The ability to divine secret messages serves this student well in later life as either a left- or right-wing fanatic crusading against smut.

THE COURT REBEL. A sheep in hyena's clothing, the Court Rebel (or Court Fool) is the school administration's officially sanctioned and sanitized revolutionary. With a substantial stake in the status quo, the CR is a self-starter whom the administration can count on to defuse any serious student unrest by trivializing the issues or attacking the wrong issue altogether. Court Rebels often make a living as public-relations counselors after graduation.

THE LUTHERAN NUN. Able to appear cloistered in the middle of the state fair midway, the LN usually majors in psychology or sociology, but only on condition that he/she be allowed to skip the parts about phalluses. Social Work is a favorite occupation of LN's, and Lithium the recreational drug of choice.

THE MYSTERIES OF THE ADMISSIONS OFFICE:
Three Inexplicable Student Categories.

"What Are *You* Doing Here?" The clearly over-qualified student with no family ties to explain why he/she enrolled in a GLC instead of some Ivy League over-achiever's heaven.

"What Am *I* Doing Here?" The irritatingly over-egoized student who is convinced that his/her uniqueness and ability (usually artistic) are as pearls cast before swine. A shrewd assessment of those skills generally keeps them where they will not be put to a severe test.

"How Did *He* Get Here?" Even by today's casual standards, this person's presence can be attributed only to computer error. Although he can sometimes redeem himself by being colorful, a'la *Animal House,* he is more often seen only as a sullen presence under the hood of his GTO, endlessly changing and rechanging the spark plugs—the only skill he is known to possess.

"Studying" in Scandinavia.

For Scandinavian/American students and their families, the pinnacle of academic success is not receiving a Ph.D., nor being appointed to a tenured professorship. The ultimate achievement is to spend part of your college career studying in Scandinavia, preferably in the country from which your ancestors came.

Even the honor of having a child spend four years on the dean's list doesn't give as much pride to a Scandinavian/ American family as being able to brag about their child who, at this very moment—right now—is studying *in Scandinavia!* Just saying it: "My kid's studying *in Scandinavia!*," well, it gives you class. What would your emigrant forebears say to hear that their descendant was at The Great University, talking with all those learned professors? And what would they say of you? You, who are prosperous enough to send him/her? Just think!

It's not just parents who go a little crazy about this sort of thing. Students also think that going to Scandinavia to study is pretty hot stuff. And it won't surprise anybody but a parent to hear that the students' plans aren't necessarily the same as their parents' plans.

Students, being the more realistic, realize that a trip is a trip, even if you do have to pay lip service to the pretense that it was undertaken solely for the purpose of academic self-improvement.

The cost, length, and status of these trips vary. One type of trip you have to pay for yourself, and the other someone else pays for via a grant or scholarship. Guess which one has the higher status.

In terms of length, you can either go for the quickie during interim semester or take the long count and stay away for a year.

The year long versions are more challenging, but troublesome because you really have to learn the language. Your grandmother's table prayer, demands for food and descriptions of bodily functions are inadequate for a solid year's communication needs. You soon learn that professors of all lands delight in the sort of exalted and jargon-ridden language that's *never* covered in a Pocket Dictionary/Complete with Menu Guide.

Because of the shortsightedness of school officials who placed interim semester in January, taking an interim tour of Scandinavia might seem like a questionable bargain. Worse still, students on these tours are chaperoned to within an inch of their lives (or past). Still, the prices can't be beat, and they can't watch you all the time, no matter how hard they try.

The following are the goals most students list in anticipation of their trip to Scandinavia. Their expectations differ slightly by gender, but they also show some remarkable similarities.

MALE	FEMALE
1. Romance	1. Shopping
2. Getting away from parents	2. Getting away from parents
3. Sightseeing	3. Sightseeing
4. Cultural enlightenment	4. Romance
5. Education	5. Education

MALE Expectations and Goals:

1. ROMANCE: Having an affair with someone with whom you cannot communicate, save by rudimentary sign language, holds a powerful appeal to young males. This is because they have not yet realized that this is the primary means of communication for most relationships.

2. GETTING AWAY FROM YOUR PARENTS: Scandinavia is thousands of miles away and seven hours time difference. This makes it very hard for your parents to check up on you. You *do* have to learn to be a better letter writer than you are now, but even then your parents will have only your word as to what you've been doing.

3. SIGHTSEEING: Interim trips are infamous for their group tours. Sightseeing, en masse, is akin to an orgy. You have to be a good team player, and even then it isn't much fun except in retrospect. Most public sights—Vigeland Park, Tivoli, Gammlastan, Thingvellir, etc. are scheduled only to reassure parents that their children's time was occupied by wholesome activities.

The things you will best remember—funky basement bars, heated arguments about politics, and exotic romances, are *definitely* not things you want to share with your family. Rest assured that they have no interest in the details.

4. CULTURAL ENLIGHTENMENT: Like every amusement for young males, the term "Cultural Enlightenment" is a euphemism for something else. In this case, "C.E." (as it will undoubtedly be dubbed) means drinking a lot of foreign beer and learning to swear in a foreign language.

It does not mean attending recorder concerts, going to weaving museums or taking notes on lectures discussing "Scandinavian Multi-National Corporations and Their Responsibilities to Third World Development Strategies." You can get that stuff at home on tape from public radio.

5. EDUCATION: Considering that you've spent all that money and come all this way to learn exactly those things which your parents and your college don't want you to learn, the least you can do is to take a stab at your course offerings. Who knows when you'll need to know all about "Urban Planning and the Cooperative Folk Tradition"?

FEMALE Expectations and Goals

1. SHOPPING: It's a shame that no college credit is offered for shopping, because shopping can provide a fast assessment of a culture with as much certainty as any report by an anthropologist, archeologist or political analyst.

As a skilled shopper/observer, you discover what a culture truly values, spot false pieties and learn much of the nation's self-image, as well as its fears. You quickly learn about tax policy, consumer patterns and pride (or lack of it) in craftsmanship and service. Best of all, you get to take home all the research.

2. GETTING AWAY FROM YOUR PARENTS: Traveling to Scandinavia is a lot like an extended Luther League trip, because it lulls your parents into thinking that you are acting far more respectably than you really are.

Since Scandinavian/American parents have never believed the stereotype of the sexy Nordic, they assume that your virtue will be much safer in Scandinavia than it would be in one of those European countries to the south, where they're all sex maniacs.

3. SIGHTSEEING: While no one would doubt the charms of winter sightseeing during an interim trip, particularly if one is kept cozy in the strong arms of a cross-country ski champion, the student who spends a full year in Scandinavia has limitless opportunities.

Even if your parents don't realize it, the rest of Europe thinks that Nordic women are unbearably sexy. What more fun than to join a student tour to someplace like Yugoslavia, where only the border guards will know your real nationality? It's like spring break in Florida, only more tasteful.

4. ROMANCE: The Scandinavian male has just about everything a Scandinavian/American woman could want in a lover or husband. He won't be a nonstop talker like American men, and Nordic males are famous for being sensitive without being touchy.

He's sure to win approval, sight-unseen, from your parents just because he's Scandinavian. And he's exotic enough so that even his bad habits can be written off to cultural diversity.

5. EDUCATION: You're bound to be asked about this, so save some notes, for Pete's sake. Borrow some if you have to, and copy them on the plane on the way home, if you can stay awake. When your parents beam and ask you what you learned, just remember that a little sincerity is all they want, not an exposé.

"Studying" in Scandinavia: What Mom and Dad don't know, won't hurt them.

The Village Idiom:

(A New Scandinavian Phrase Book From Misinformation Language Services, Inc., AB, A/S.)

One of the delights of traveling in Scandinavia is that most of the people there speak very good English. People in other European countries also often speak English, but they hate to admit it. Scandinavians don't mind speaking any language that will separate a tourist from his or her money.

If you're planning a trip, you've probably already looked for a decent phrase book. Most foreign-language phrase books say things like "Pardon me, but is this an establishment at which I can buy and/or purchase either/or petrol by-products and/or pre-packaged foodstuffs?"

Nobody you know talks like that in English—are you sure you want to talk like that in a foreign language? Does it surprise you that the locals ignore you when you talk like that?

What you really need are phrases that make you sound less like a fool and more like a native. Take this book with you to Scandinavia, and point out the phrase you want to communicate. You'll be a big hit, and probably even draw a small crowd.

These phrases have been translated into the very latest and finest idiomatic Swedish available. We have chosen Swedish because every literate Scandinavian can read Swedish—even if the pronunciation may give them some trouble. If they don't seem to understand at first, talk louder. If they still don't understand, shout.

Translator's note: Much of the delight of studying foreign

peoples lies in learning what whimsical and foolish figures of speech these people manage to come up with, and how far their little idioms are from what they're actually trying to say in plain English.

For those of you who enjoy such subtle semantic amusements, we have printed a *literal* translation of each Swedish idiom at the end of each section. No matter how "kooky" or "Way Out" some of those literal translations may sound, you must *trust* us that those Swedish phrases mean exactly what we say they do. Honest!

IN PUBLIC

1. "Please help me change these traveler's checks into kronor."

   Jag är en galen amerikansk bov. Ge mig alla dina pengar.

   "Yah air en yalen ah-mehr-ee-cahn-sk bohv. Gay may ahl-la deen-a peng-gahr."

2. "Excuse me, Miss. May I assist you in carrying your shopping parcels?"

   Din Kropp glöder med värme, och jag är en svag man.

   "Din Krowp glue-dehr med vair-meh, oh yah air en svahg mahn."

3. "Waitperson, this is not the menu item which we indicated. Perhaps you inadvertently bestowed upon us another diner's foodstuffs."

   Nycktra till dig ditt djävla avskum, annars ska jag skicka dig till nästa fredsstyrka för att ta hand om alla avvikare!

   "Nick-trah teel day dit yahv-lah ahv-skoom, ahn-narsh skah yah sheek-ah day teel ness-tah frayds-stewr-ka foor aht tah hahnd ohm ahl-la ahv-veek-ahr-eh!"

4. "Is this the way to Vigeland Park/Tivoli/Gammlastan/Thingvellir? I'm so anxious to see your Cultural Treasures!"

   Vigeland/Tivoli/Gammlastan/Thingvellir är dom mest värdlösa platser jag nånsin har sett. Ni borde offra mig fri sex och knark för att få mig ditt igen.

"_____ air dohm mest vair-deh-loos-ah plahts-er yah known-seen har set. Nee bore-deh ohf-frah may free sex oh k-narc foor aht foh may deet ee-yen."

5. "I just *love* the bargains I get when I shop in your fine stores!"
   Djävla fan vad allt är dyrt!
   "Yev-lah fahn vahd ahllt air deart!"

PLODDINGLY LITERAL, IDIOM TO IDIOM TRANSLATIONS OF "IN PUBLIC" PHRASES:

1. I am a crazed American Gangster. Give me all your kroner.
2. Your body glows with temptation, and I am a weak man.
3. Shape up, pond scum, or I'll make sure you're part of the next U.N. peacekeeping force to the nasties.
4. Vigeland Park/Tivoli/Gammlastan/Thingvellir is the most worthless thing I've ever seen. You people would have to offer me free sex and drugs to get me to go there again.
5. Hellfire and Damnation, all this crap is overpriced!

AT YOUR RELATIVES

1. "Thank you for the wonderful meal! No one can make herring and eel parts into as tasty a dish as you can!"
   Jag har ätit värre mat i lumpen! Och där behövde jag inte vara så artig.
   "Yah hahr et-tit vair-reh maht ee loomp-pen! Oh dair bay-hoov-deh yah een-teh vah-rah so ahr-teeg."

2. "Your hospitality is heartwarming. I will forever treasure the many mementos you have so generously given to me."
   Vad ska jag göra med alla dom här grejorna? Det finns inte en bra sak i hela den här lådan full av skit.
   "Yahd skah yah you-rah med ahl-ah dohm hair grey-your-nah? Deht feens een-teh en brah sahk ee hey-lah den hair load-ahn fool ahv schweet."

3. "I can hardly wait to express to my American family how high is my regard for all our Scandinavian relatives!"
   Dricker alla Nordiskar på det här sättet, eller är det bara du som är nersupen?
   "Deek-ehr ahl-lah Nor-deesk-ahr poh deht hair set-tet, eller air

deht bahr-rah doo sohm air nair-soop-pen?

4. "I certainly can't comprehend how my ancestors could ever have left such a wonderful place as this!"

Jag är färvånad att mina förfäder stannade i den här förgätna hålan så länge som de gjorde!

"Yah air fair-vohn-nahd aht meen-ah fair-fed-er stahn-na-deh ee den hair foor-yet-nah hole-ahn so lehng-eh sohm day your-deh!"

5. "Thank you, Aunt ＿＿＿＿＿/Uncle ＿＿＿＿＿ for the wonderful visit! Are there any members of our extended family in America to whom you would wish me to extend your personal greetings?"

Hörru du, Moster ＿＿＿＿/Farbror＿＿＿＿, du ser du ut som en tjuv! Är du säker på att du inte varit i fängelse för stjäla änkor och förlorade barn?

"Hoor-roo doo, Mohs-ter ＿＿＿＿/Fahr-bror ＿＿＿＿, soo sair doo oot sohm schoov. Air doo sek-er poh aht doo een-teh vahr-eet ee feng-el-seh foor st'yell-nah eng-kohr oh foor-lohr-ah-deh bahrn?"

PLODDINGLY LITERAL, IDIOM TO IDIOM TRANSLATION OF "AT YOUR RELATIVES" PHRASES:

1. I've eaten worse food in the army. And there I didn't have to be polite about it.
2. What am I going to do with all this crap? There isn't a decent thing in this whole box of cheap trinkets.
3. Do all Scandinavians drink like that, or is it just you that has a terminal drinking problem?
4. I'm surprised my ancestors stayed in this forsaken place as long as they did!
5. Well now, Aunt ＿＿＿＿/Uncle ＿＿＿＿, you look like crooks to me. Are you sure you haven't been to prison for robbing widows and orphans?

ROMANTIC SITUATIONS:

1. "It has been heavenly to spend time with you. May I see you again soon?"

Var jag kommer ifrån skulle vi tvinga en så tjok som du att banta. Tror du inte du skulle må bättre om du gjorde det?

"Vahr yah kohm-mer ee-frohn school-eh vee t'veeng-gah en so shook sohm doo aht bahn-tah. Troor doo een-ten doo school-eh moe bet-teh-reh ohm doo your-deh deht?"

2. "I don't think anybody is as sexually attractive as a Scandinavian."

Det är sant alla ni skandinaver bara pratar och aldrig gör nåt.

"Deht air sahnt aht ahl-lah nee skadn-deh-nah-ver bahr-rah prahter oh ahl-dreeg yoor note."

3. "Take me in your arms and hold me forever!"

Det är bara ett varsår.

"Deht air bahr-rah eht vahr-soar."

4. "I truly admire your intellectual and spiritual qualities.''

Jag vill slicka svettet från din kropp.

"Yah veel sleek-ah svet-tet frohn deen krohp."

5. "On my honor as an American tourist, I promise to write faithfully to you when I get home!"

Jag pratar inte svenska.

"Yah prah-tahr een-teh sven-skah."

PLODDINGLY LITERAL, IDIOM TO IDIOM TRANSLATION OF "ROMANTIC SITUATIONS" PHRASES:

1. Where I come from, we'd put someone as fat as you on a strict diet. Wouldn't you feel better about yourself if you lost weight?
2. It's really true that you Scandinavians are all talk and no show!
3. It's really just a cold sore.
4. I want to lick the sweat off your body.
5. What, me? Speak Swedish?

ABOVE:
Good Scandinavian/American
Occupation: Lutefisk Distributer

RIGHT:
Good Scandinavian/American
Occupation: Retail Sweet Corn Sales

Good Nordic Jobs

Time to Make Something of Yourself.

fter you've put in your four years at a Good Lutheran College, the next step is to go right out and find a Good Job so your mother and aunts can brag about it.

Good Jobs, like Good Colleges, are judged by the percentages of Scandinavian/Americans they offer contact with on a day to day basis. Of course, the very best jobs are those where you come into contact with practically nobody. When someone says, "He's practically working for himself," you know that person doesn't have to answer a lot of stupid questions. For all that matters, he probably doesn't have to *answer to* anybody, and he is surely the envy of the family.

Scandinavian/Americans make a different set of demands on their jobs than other folks do. For instance, we do not demand that our jobs give us fellowship. We get enough of that sort of thing at church, particularly with these new ministers who want you to turn around in the pew all the time and shake some stranger's hand every Sunday.

We assume that job satisfaction means having to deal only with a small number of regular customers or coworkers. Who could possibly find satisfaction in the chaos of having to deal with new people all the time?

The most important job recognition for Scandinavian/Americans comes from their own families. There is no more cherished job recognition than in overhearing one great-uncle tell another, "You know, Jon Mark—Waldemar's boy—got himself a nice job. His aunt told me that he sells a lot of those things he makes to the Scandinavians, and he and his wife go back there every couple of years!"

Here then, are some guidelines for finding (or avoiding) Scandinavians in the workplace.

"Do They Serve Lefse in the Company Cafeteria?":
Non-negotiable Scandinavian/American Job Demands.

Are some jobs uniquely Scandinavian/American, in the way that running a kosher deli is pretty much a Jewish preserve? Or the Episcopalian ministry is a WASP's nest? I think so.

What makes a job field attractive to Scandinavian/ Americans?What do we look for in a career, and what do we avoid? Here are some basic Nordic employment guidelines.

The Nordic Workplace:
A GOOD Job for a Scandinavian/American
is one where:

1. You can work for days without saying anything and nobody gets suspicious or upset.
2. The coffee urn is always full, and the company buys the coffee.
3. The job has enough status that you are not required to wear a company hat.
4. Technical skills are more highly valued than customer contact skills.
5. The job description leans heavily on "sincerity" and is vague about any other qualifications.
6. The office is too small for the boss to draw up an organizational chart.
7. You have autonomy. Autonomy means never having to say you're sorry. To anybody.

THE ONE-MINUTE CAREER COUNSELOR:
Good and Bad Jobs for Scandinavian/Americans.

GOOD JOBS

1. Lutefisk distributor
2. Farming
3. Retail sweet corn sales (either stand or truck)
4. Logger
5. Insurance sales (especially Lutheran Brotherhood and Sons of Norway)
6. Lutheran minister
7. Outboard motor repair
8. Resort owner
9. Lighthouse keeper
10. Scientific researcher
11. Snowmobile designer
12. Designer of sew-it-yourself clothes
13. Short order cook
14. Snowplowing/car-starting service
15. Ski instructor
16. Wildlife artist
17. Baker
18. Commercial fisherman
19. Northwoods fishing guide
20. Live-bait-and-tackle-shop owner

BAD JOBS

1. Talk show host
2. Gossip columnist
3. Arts commentator/critic

4. Disco DJ
5. Game Show host

6. Primal-scream therapist
7. Gigolo
8. Auctioneer
9. Host of literary salon
10. Chamber of commerce executive
11. Stand-up comedian
12. New-wave fashion designer

13. Haute cuisine chef
14. Sales-convention M.C.

15. Used car salesman
16. Conceptual artist
17. Restaurant reviewer
18. Elementary-school bus driver
19. Tour group guide
20. Record company executive

8. The reception room magazines are *Field and Stream, The Lutheran Standard, Popular Mechanics, Scientific American,* and *National Geographic.*
9. Your hands work with more than paper.
10. Your trendiest coworker finds a "funky little eatery," and it turns out to be the neighborhood bar where your grandfather used to eat lunch.
11. You only go indoors to warm up.

A BAD Job for a Scandinavian/American is one where:

1. Instead of a coffee break, everybody in the office holds a support group to share their feelings.
2. You have to talk amiably with total strangers just as if you'd known them for years.
3. You have to explain things more than once to coworkers or clients.
4. Your coworkers consider you hopelessly behind the times if you have not heard of a trend before the *Minneapolis Star and Tribune* writes an article about it.
5. The most successful people in the office all act, look and talk like TV game show hosts.
6. The boss wears a gold chain with a puka bead instead of a necktie and quotes Kahil Gibran extensively.
7. You have to appear exclusively loyal to more than one manager and/or client at a time.
8. The reception room magazines are *Vanity Fair, Cosmopolitan, Gentlemen's Quarterly, New York,* and *After Dark.*
9. You are the only one in the office who knows—or cares—about Syttendemai or Svenskarnasdag.
10. You do not get a paid vacation on Leif Ericsson's Day.
11. Trendiness is a job qualification, not a personal quirk.

PILGRIM'S PROGRESS EDITION: *The Changing Lutheran Ministry.*

Everything in the world changes, even—amazingly—the Lutheran Ministry. Granted, it's been at a glacial pace, but one must remember how much of the world a glacier has to push in

IF YOU THOUGHT THE MERGER WAS BAD ENOUGH,
WAIT TILL YOU SEE THE NEW WAVE MINISTERS.

front of it whenever it wants to shift a little. As many reformers have found, it's easier to move a minister than it is to push an entire congregation into something new and untested.

But there have been changes. Sometimes we're the last to see them because we are so close to our own churches and ministers that we can't step back far enough to get a good perspective. Here are some of the more noticeable changes in the past few decades.

THEN	NOW
Luther League retreats	Christian community ashrams
Walk for Mankind	Marathon for Central Ameria
Lutefisk suppers	Food shelves
Hosting the regional Luther League convention	Sponsoring juvenile chemical-dependency counseling centers
Assured lifetime tenure	Only the luckiest seminarians even get a call from a parish
Minister's *real* job was to raise enough money to build a new church	Minister's *real* job is to raise enough money to maintain church buildings in need of repair
Parishioners were lost to Sunday morning golf games and fishing	Parishioners are lost to Sunday morning TV preachers
"Setting an Example" meant never smoking or drinking, staying faithful to your wife and practically never smiling	"Setting an Example" means offering political asylum, boycotting the appropriate companies and countries, and not getting divorced without a good reason
"Missionary Efforts" meant Africa. Period.	"Missionary Efforts" means outreach to racial, sexual and ethnic minorities
Continual attacks from the Left and intellectuals for being an intellectual anachronism, and/or a pusher of the Opiate of the Masses	Continual attacks from the Right and fundamentalists for being an anti-Christ, false prophet, Commie-dupe, pervert lover, human rights weeper, and baby killer

Logging in a Polyurethane World

The natural element of Scandinavians is wood. They are surrounded by it, and they carve it into wondrous forms for furniture, homes, utensils and decorations.

When the great waves of Scandinavian immigrants came to America, it was no surprise that they gravitated to the areas with wood industries.

America was also a nation dominated by wood. People ate at a wooden table and sat on a wooden chair that was set on a wood floor in a wood house. Then they hitched their horse to a wooden wagon and went visiting.

You don't need to be a brilliant observer of social trends to realize that that day has passed. A young couple today will likely eat at a hi-tech table of glass and polyurethane-coated metal, in their new condominium made of prefabricated concrete modules. They will then climb into their car with its fiberglass panels and go shopping for an antique brass bed—for nostalgia's sake.

No one has been hit harder by this change in the logging industry than Scandinavian/Americans. For us, it is not only an occupational loss but a cultural loss as well—comparable only to the loss Pamplona would suffer if it had no more bulls to run.

For Scandinavians, the forest was the source of all myth and all materials. From its mighty oaks, they crafted their long dragonships to harry distant coasts.

One of the early Viking strategic theorists, Knut Hardoak, even postulated that since the finest spear shafts were of oak, it followed logically that the best spear points would also be made of oak. He nearly bankrupt his little kingdom outfitting his warriors entirely with state-of-the-art wooden spears and swords, before setting out to harry the Norman coast.

Unfortunately, Knut had spent so much money on what had come to be known as his "Spruce-Wars" weapons systems that he had no funds left for mundane matters like hiring a navigator or training his crews. Anything that did not fit into his

Chopping away at Gender Roles: Paul Bunyan meets his match. ▶

preconceived strategies (like tides, winds, and weather) was ignored.

His invincible force of "purely defensive" Viking ships was almost immediately blown off course, and ran aground on a small island in the Orkneys. There, they were treacherously attacked and defeated in a pitched battle (which lasted nearly a quarter of an hour) by a fierce force of 17 peasants, a nun and a very large sheep dog.

More peaceful developments in wood use came around 1789, when Jon-Olav Jon-Olavssson established the first industrial sawmill in the town of Trädheimstul. Jon-Olav had grown up in Trädheimstul, watching the village women laboriously making the traditional trädskor and trädskjortar (clogs and wooden shirts). While one woman planed the wood into smooth sheets, others bent them over patterns, and still others rosemaled traditional patterns onto the finished shirts. The whole process was supposed to be a closely guarded women's mystery, but Jon-Olav was an inquisitive lad with a quick mind and an outstanding ability to peek through log cracks—an ability that later got him in serious trouble with the parson's daughter, Synnøve the Soft.

Years later, Jon-Olav returned to his childhood home a rich man, though he never mentioned exactly where he had gotten all that money. Jon-Olav had never forgotten the back-breaking labor of the village women as they planed and hammered away at those wooden shirts intended for the backs of rich people elsewhere.

More to the point, Jon-Olav had never forgotten how the women looked through the chinks in the logs—their powerful arms rippling with a forest worker's muscles; their blond bodies glistening with sweat; the smell of sweat, perfume, and pine sap mixing in his pubescent nostrils, and so on, and so on.

Deeply moved by these memories, and dedicated to helping as many women as possible, Jon-Olav established the Jon-Olav Jon-Olavssson Trädskjortar Sawmill and Home for Wayward Girls.

The modern equipment Jon-Olav brought in allowed the

village women to increase their production of wooden shirts till they were exporting to every town and village in Scandinavia. Even today, many American families treasure an heirloom trädskjorta brought to America by a distant ancestor whose name the family cannot remember.

An interesting footnote: With the prosperity the Sawmill brought to Trädheimstul, the village women, led by Synnøve, quickly pooled their resources, bought out Jon-Olav and had him committed.

In 1947, the Social-Democrat Government established the Hjemlandet Trädskjorta Folk Museum in Trädheimstul, being very careful never to actually mention Jon-Olav by name in the proclamation.

The Museum now boasts the largest collection of wooden shirts to be found anywhere in the world. The museum is open all summer, and by appointment in the winter. Your travel agent can give you details of tours and fares.

Who Lives on a Farm Nowadays?

The media have given a lot of attention belatedly to farmers, and, happily most of it has taken the form of unromantic examinations of rural economic problems. The media usually swing from *Saturday Evening Post*-style sentimental reveries about grandma's kitchen to genuine urban shock at the discovery that there is more poverty in the country than there is in the ghettos.

So, somewhere outstate, between these two extremes, are the real people who live on farms. Who are they? Who really lives on a farm nowadays?

Axel Fredrickson

Old Farmer

MAKES:
Corn and soybeans
Some wheat
Tried sunflowers, but that didn't
work too good

READS:
Soybean Grower's Journal
The Lutheran Standard
Weekly church bulletin

COMMENTS:
"My great grandfather came from
Lande, in Sweden, in 1872, and
bought this land from the U.S. government and the railroad company.
That was just after the Sioux was
defeated at Fort Ridgely and New
Ulm. My great-uncle Oscar said he
used to see some of them around
here down by the corncrib once in a
while, but not too much,
really . . ."

Eric Halvorson
Krs Nordgren
Yuppie Investors

MAKE:
$120,000 a year combined adjusted
income (pre-tax)

READ:
Architectural Digest
The New York Times
Dow Jones News Service
Wall Street Journal
Bon Appétit
Travel & Leisure
Forbes
Vanity Fair
Connoisseur

COMMENTS:
"When we saw this property coming back from vacation, and it was
like a third of what you'd pay for a
similar investment anywhere else in
the state, we just couldn't pass it up
for a little get-away, even though all
the poverty is really depressing.
The Agribusiness infrastructure has
got to take up the slack pretty soon,
although that probably won't help
all the people around here. I suppose most of them will just have to
move somewhere else. That will be
inconvenient for them, of course,
but it's also bound to draw even
more investment interest once the
land prices really bottom out."

"Vic"
(No last name given)
Survivalist/Prophet

MAKES:
Very little trouble for his neighbors,
till one day . . .

READS:
Soldier of Fortune
The Prophecy Newsletter
The White-Man's Guidebook

COMMENTS:
"Get off my telephone line! This is
private property! I'll make a citi-
zen's arrest if you don't get off right
now! Listen, scumbag, do you
know what kind of damage an M79
Grenade Launcher could do to that
little Jap car I bet you own..."

Jim Torgerson (Moonman)
Jane Olson (Sunflower)
Residual Hippies

MAKE:
Pottery for Renaissance Fair, poetry for small literary journals. Jane is "into" Daycare.

READ:
Mother Jones
Rolling Stone
The Progressive

COMMENTS:
"We actually only own like one-fifth of this place, because a long time ago I was one of five guys who started the Northern Lights Commune, you know. We still pay some rent to the other guys, but the only one who's a real hassle is Tom, who's a C.P.A. now, and always was a real narc and a bummer. I mean, anybody who could do as much acid as he did and never have a single flashback is just an uptight butthole, you know, man..."

Bob and Charleene
Skogstrand
Exurban Pioneers

MAKE:
130 mile daily roundtrip to work in Twin Cities.

READ:
Saturday Evening Post
New England Magazine
Better Homes and Gardens

COMMENTS:
"Both Charleene and I grew up on farms, but there aren't really any jobs for Project Engineers in small towns, so we try to combine the best of both worlds. I suppose that in a few years this will all be inner city for Minneapolis, with the, uh, sort of people, you know, and all the problems that they drag along. But if that ever happens, we'll just buy some land that's a couple hours further out, or maybe I'll be ready to retire and we can really move far enough away from those people."

David and Beth
Lundgren
Young Farmers

MAKE:
16% loan payments on devalued farm land

READ:
SBA pamphlets
FmHA foreclosure proceedings
Bankruptcy court records

COMMENTS:
"We're the fourth generation to farm this land, and we may be the ones who have the honor to lose it to the government. That's kind of funny because my Great-Grandfather left Sweden when his older brother inherited the farm, and he had nothing to farm. Maybe I should change the milking parlor into a bingo parlor to make some quick bucks. I'm a born gambler—I'm a farmer, ain't I?"

ns in the
oth coun-
, as well
interme-
Reagan

steps to prevent future starvation and to lift the continent out of the poverty that afflicts millions of its people and saddles many of them with the lowest incomes on earth.

leery of formal commitments to provide $46 billion in additional aid and between $35 billion and $55 billion in relief of existing debt, two major elements of the plan.

co
ci
str
tri
as
di
sa

erts said
the over-
nuclear
SALT II
iolations
reaty, in-
ent of a
ballistic
orbidden
encoding
terconti-

ed there
viet non-
I Treaty
Missile
Test Ban
ical and
of 1972,
Chemical
Helsinki
rights).
probably
hreshold

etire the
based on
and mil-
not an
nce with
esult.

okesman
ement of
"an eco-
d not an
npliance.
vessels
istration
time that
ve to re-

, a lead-
ol, inter-
nnounce-
d news."
n to dis-
said the
lk about
uld only
from the
a state-
be the
rotecting
for new
s."

New Example of Government Interference!

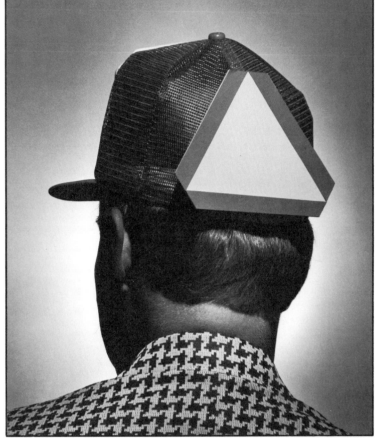

The Minnesota Legislature recently passed a bill requiring all Scandinavian/Americans to wear a reflective SMV (Slow Moving Vehicle) sign on the front and rear of their caps when entering a Humorous Zone to avoid a collision with a fast-moving witticism.

How much longer are Scandinavian/Americans going to stand for this sort of treatment?

Th
the
all
we
ag
of
clu
see
mi
"e
of
ne

In
ha
co
of
Tr
Tr
To
the
We
Fi
Re
als
Te

Re
Po
co
ita
eff
SA

Si
La
the
no
eff
Th
we
off
it
fu

Se
ing
pre
me
He
ma
ad
ab
in
Kr
me
on
us

His counterpart for the Group of 77, Raif Dizdarevic, foreign secretary of Yugoslavia, said the organization views the program "with full understanding and support." Outside assistance by donors is of "crucial importance." They are, he said, "rightfully

Edgard Pisani of France spoke in favor of a report endorsing the Africa program, which has been bottled up for several weeks in the session's preparatory committee. Pisani, committee chairman, said that donor countries, in agreeing last December

Comic Relief
for the Stoic Masses.

What can you say about a group that thinks that lutefisk is funny, let alone edible? The truth is, when we're by ourselves we're a pretty funny bunch, or at least we seem to be. Maybe it's just the lack of jocular competition that makes us seem funny then. Or perhaps it's a form of sensory deprivation that magnifies the slightest glimmer of levity into a major merriment.

Scandinavian/American humor is based on hardship. You can actually make Scandinavian/Americans laugh after a mishap has happened (happened to you, by the way, not to them) simply by saying "Uff Da!"

Example: On your wedding day, before the wedding pictures have been taken, you spill grape juice all over your white gown or tux. Everybody inhales till there is a severe oxygen shortage, but no one says a thing. Certainly no one laughs!

Then, after tense milliseconds, you simply say, "Uff Da." Nothing more. No funny facial expressions. And everybody cracks up like you had just turned into Mark Twain.

Why is this funny? A horrible thing has happened, but we Scandinavian/Americans know that our lives are played out on the very edge of clinical depression, and any time we face a horrible situation and don't plunge into depression or go out and shoot ourselves in classical Nordic fashion, it's a time to let go and have a good laugh.

All the same, you will notice that the chapter on Scandinavian/American Humor is the shortest in the book. You'll just have to learn to cherish what's there.

Behave Yourself!:
Times It's Not Appropriate To Be Funny.

During dull church services.
At the wedding of a pregnant relative.
At church suppers when the minister is at your table.
Anytime during confirmation class.
During funerals of very old relatives you never met.
When your spouse or parents are preparing their taxes.
The first three weeks of a diet.
During the formal ceremony at a family reunion.
When the uncles are discussing politics.
When the aunts are discussing the morals of today's youth.
During Svenskarnasdag.
During Norway Day.
Anytime they're singing songs from the old country.
When your Aunt sings in church, no matter how off-key.
During a discussion of Bergman's films.
During Luther League get-togethers with out-of-town churches.
When the kid in Luther League who gets all misty when he/she reads
    from *The Prophet* gets up to hold devotions.
During graduation ceremonies at Lutheran colleges.
During baccalaureate services at Lutheran colleges.
During chapel services at Lutheran colleges.
During sincere group discussions at Lutheran colleges.
During modern dance recitals based on religious themes.
During losing Football/Basketball/etc., games at Lutheran colleges.
During losing Football/Basketball/etc., seasons at Lutheran colleges.
During the spring student art fair.
During a mime performance.
When relatives show pictures of distant foreign relatives you have
    never met, and never will.
When uncles show pictures of their latest hunting trip, complete with
    disembowled deer/bear/caribou/etc.
When they tell you how good the fishing was years ago.
When they tell you how terrible everything has gotten in the past few
    years.

When they explain the government to you in depth.

When they explain their religious ideas to you in depth.

When they tell you how terrible welfare is because our ancestors started without government handouts (forgetting the nearly free land).

When they compete to offend every racial/sexual/preferential/religious and ethnic subgroup you know.

Whenever you're with the grownups.

BEQUEST DENIED

MUSEUM BEQUEST REFUSED!
Mrs. Beverly Offerdahl was very upset when the Swedish Institute refused her bequest of her entire collection of souvenir snow-shaker scenes, collected over many years during her travels across the entire United States and Canada!

Nordic Entertainments:

How Do You Amuse a Scandinavian/American?

Y ou cannot amuse a Scandinavian/American. Scandinavian/Americans amuse themselves in ways that are sure to confound even the most insightful and understanding outside observer.

Consistent with our overall behavior, we choose amusements that reward isolation and silence, and are depressing. Our only active sport is eating while arguing with our families.

Scandinavian/Americans love to argue with their families because it allows them to show off their stubbornness. We're stubborn and uncompromising with everybody, of course, but we're nagged by the fear that outsiders may not recognize our obstinacy as a magnificent achievement.

Scandinavian/Americans believe that sport, like the life which it mirrors, ought to hurt. Being a Viking fan hurts, and skiing does very little except hurt, either from falling down or from freezing to death.

We love to argue about taxes—in public even—because that hurts so good too. Few people in today's lively debate about Minnesota's tax and business policies recall the uproar over the 1962 Great Scales Tax Scare, but we'd like to refresh everyone's memory on the issue.

Here, then, are some of the major sports of Scandinavian/American life.

FISHING:
RELAXING, OR COMA-INDUCING?

Fishing comes in three forms: ice, boat, and dock. All three rely on sensory deprivation for their entertainment value, except that you're generally colder when you're ice fishing.

ICE FISHING

Ice fishing is the only form of abuse that does not get you into trouble with the law in Minnesota. This is because it is self-inflicted and because there are practical limits to the percentages of the population that can be put in jail.

There are two forms of ice fishing. Pure—or Unprotected—Ice Fishing involves only the individual fisherman, a hole in the ice that is constantly refreezing (a little hint from Mother Nature that fishermen seldom heed) and a piece of string.

Philosophers say that Pure Ice Fishing is a form of Scando/Zen meditation where the pilgrim contemplates the oneness of the Universe and the numbness of his body parts.

Ethnologists say that the Unprotected Ice Fisherman is expressing a subconscious solidarity with the ethnic archetypes of his heritage. In English, this only means that he is freezing to death, just as his ancestor, Gorm the Very Cold, did in 734, near what later became Stavanger.

The other form of ice fishing—Protected Ice Fishing—gets its name from the huts the fishermen build to shelter themselves from both the cold and women. In fact, Protected Ice Fishing is really an excuse for grown men to play house. Not only do they play house, they play town.

When the local lake's ice reaches proper thickness, men hop into their pickups and drag their huts to a seasonally permanent location. Other men see these first huts and soon the lake has so many huts that regular streets and avenues have formed, occasionally complete with street markers.

And there you have it: an instant town—but a town just as some men have fantasized it since their boyhoods—a self-regulating town with no bureaucrats and very few women.

These ice houses are decorated by men, for men. They feature no frilly craft-items found in supermarket magazines, no cheery pastels

Ice Fishing: The only form of abuse which does not get you into trouble with the law in Minnesota.

and no hanging things made of yarn. The ice fishing house is the modern version of the Victorian hunting lodge. If ice houses today look more like the inside of a van than a grand lodge, you must bear in mind that neither the great wealth nor the fine Victorian sensibilities that built those old lodges are commonly to be found nowadays.

While ice fishing houses do offer some improvement over sitting exposed to the elements on the ice pack, balancing the primal forces of frostbite against tribal starvation, it has been my experience that ice houses are still not all that comfortable.

While I understand that being a little uncomfortable is an important part of the celebration of maleness, I have always been tempted to celebrate my maleness in my perfectly warm house, with nice soft chairs, and just lie about how uncomfortable I was.

Instead of bundling up like a fool on a polar bear hunt, I could just ask my wife to go to a movie for a few hours because I wanted to be alone.

Then I could call some guys up, and tell them to drive over in pickups so we'd all feel real macho. We'd just hang out at the house, have a few beers, pass the afternoon lying about how uncomfortable we were, and congratulate each other on how well we were taking it.

We'd stay warm, save the gas money to drive to the lake, and spare ourselves the terror of listening to the ice crack every time a pickup drove near our ice house.

I suppose there's a catch to this plan somewhere, but it sure makes sense to me.

BOAT FISHING

Boat fishing is a religious experience for Scandinavian/Americans, containing as it does the four sacred elements of Nordic life: water, silence, isolation and inertia.

Perhaps it would be recognized for the folk religion it truly is if we were to invite anthropologists and National Geographic photographers to observe our annual spring pilgrimages, where parades of boats on their trailers wind through such shrine towns as Walker, Biwabik and Alexandria.

Like every good religion, we have developed elaborate methods of judging the sincerity and faith of our fellow worshippers. We feel, for instance, that one of the most visible and outward signs of an inward and invisible fishing grace is the outboard motor.

The truly righteous outboard has about as much horsepower as a Cuisinart. The pure at heart don't *need* any more. Only those still in the bondage of noise and speed want more.

The virtuous outboard is an old motor, handed down from parent to child, with its paint long since worn off or bleached out by the sun.

By owning an old motor, you display two important Scandinavian/American virtues: 1) You obviously take care of your things, and/or are able to repair things which the spendthrift or novelty-seeker would long ago have discarded, and 2) You come from an old and established fishing family.

Although the standards are less rigorous, Scandinavian/Americans *do* judge other people by their boats. While we realize that the all-important thing is that people are out there fishing in the boat of their choice; and while we *do* realize that marine economics and supply have changed over the years, we still believe that no one will ever cross that great final river to heaven in an aluminum boat.

The lead boat to heaven will certainly be a wooden boat—mahogany colored and varnished till it gleams—with a substantial wooden bow cap. As a child, I always thought that those bow caps were simply places for me to go when I was feeling queasy, or wishing I had something exciting to do. Crawling over three adults on my way up to the bow usually gave me all the excitement and attention I could stand for several hours.

Now I find that those bow caps are symbols and tools of seafaring ability. A boat with a bow cap can head into wind and waves which would send a flat-bottomed swamp skiff to the bottom. A person with a good bow cap is a true north Atlantic sea-faring Viking, and not some swamp-scooting southerner or prairie admiral.

As with motors, so with boats: Older boats are better than new boats. It's a proven fact that fish won't come near a shiny, new boat—they have their pride too. Who wants to get caught by a beginner or a dilettante?

The unpardonable fishing sin for Scandinavian/Americans is to put a big, overpowered outboard—the kind with the huge powerhouse taller than a small child—on your boat and go hotrodding all over the lake making lots of noise. Most people assume that those who behave that way are simply too drunk to hotrod within the confines of a highway.

Finally, there is the ethical issue of electronics. I recently went fishing on a boat with more electronic gear than a nuclear submarine. We had range finders, depth finders, things that went ping and things that looked like they were looking for Russian missiles. We knew all about that lake's depth, water temperature and rate of flow. We could tell where the fish were, where they had been and where they were headed. I wouldn't have been surprised to learn we could check to see if they had a police record as well.

All we didn't have were fish. They had lived around Scandinavian/Americans long enough to know that keeping your mouth shut was the only way to survive.

That was just as well. The failure of his expensive bells-and-whistles system depressed our host so much that he didn't say a word all afternoon. The rest of us enjoyed the day, and he finally learned what fishing is all about.

DOCK FISHING

Fishing off the dock is a great Scandinavian/American sports metaphor because it is nothing but desolation covered by the thinnest veneer of entertainment.

Consider: People walk by themselves to the ends of docks only to A) jump off and end it all, B) rendezvous with an enemy submarine to be whisked away to who-knows-what evil empire, or C) catch under-sized panfish with a bamboo pole. All three of these are acts of desperation.

On the positive side, your back seldom hurts as much when you are dock fishing as when you are boat fishing. Best of all, you can walk away from the dock any time to do something interesting.

My grandmother used to march me down to the shores of Lake Blackduck when I was a child. There we would fish for sunfish for supper. Her favorite dock was a pontoon dock, which bobbed erratically. The only time I have ever been truly seasick was on that blasted dock.

My grandmother probably never heard of haiku (since Martin Luther never wrote any), but I would like to dedicate this Nordic haiku to her and her boring sport:

> To fish with bamboo pole
> at dock's end
> teaches patience,
> but Lord, it's dull!

Eating and Arguing
With Your Family.

Scandinavian/Americans' favorite sport is a biathlon event, combining Olympic-class eating, and free-style arguing with the family. If this seems to contradict our Nordic stereotype as a bunch of nonverbal, nondemonstrative stoics, it is simply because no outsider has ever been invited to one of these private spectacles.

Even in our arguments, Scandinavian/Americans do not believe in confrontation. We practice the trickle-down method of criticism. Example: Rather than criticize Paul and Kirstin's childrearing techniques to their face, we tell their cousin, or aunt, and let *them* tell Paul and Kirstin what we said.

The jaded non-Scandinavian may hint that our arguments, like our food, lack the spicy heat that brings tears to one's eyes. We feel, however, that neither food nor arguments have to be dangerous to command your attention.

Scandinavian/American food is not a stunning artistic creation prepared by gaunt men who take a near-Zen approach to artichokes. It is a committee effort prepared by fat little cooks with raging enthusiasms for big servings.

Likewise, Scandinavian/American arguments are no less heartfelt simply because they lack fistfights and small arms fire. We do not believe in making operatic gestures, nor in screaming till we are hoarse. But it is hard to imagine an argument more intense than one that can smolder for years, breaking again into open flame at every family get-together.

When I was at college, I dated the student who ran the college's antiquated switchboard, whose pull cords had to be continually plugged and unplugged. This taught me the skill of freezing a conversation in mid-sentence when the switchboard lit up, and the ability to resume that sentence without losing a syllable when she was free again.

It took incredible concentration to carry on a conversation like that, but I soon realized that this was the same skill my family carried into their marathon arguments. Aunts and uncles who had not seen each other for six months could, after a few minutes of greetings, resume an old argument in midsentence. That particular argument may have been started four get-togethers ago, which meant that they had all been thinking and stewing about it the entire time.

And what was it exactly that we argued about? Being practical people, we avoided philosophy and argued practical ideas. That was not intellectual sloth, but brilliant strategy. We needed some leeway for disagreement, because we had to live with each other. Philosophical questions are incapable of resolution, or even compromise, but any practical application of such abstracts exists *only* in the realm of compromise. Thus we could argue without excommunicating.

My uncle put it more bluntly: "Philosophy is too rich a soil to grow anything useful in. You'll just burn out the roots." At least, that's the gist of what he said. I was in college then, and was very excited about the opportunities to introduce words like *eschatology, perspicacious* and *traducianism* into every argument. That sort of behavior is seldom rewarded in Scandinavian/American families.

It's been quite a while since I was in college, and I still haven't had a chance to use any of those words. But I have attended many family arguments in some seven Scandinavian/American families, and the good—or bad—news is that we all argue about basically the same things in basically the same way.

Scandinavian/Americans argue alphabetically. We argue about whose Ancestors were better, and who got the Breaks. Church affairs are always ripe for an argument, as are Domestic issues. Expenses are debated on both an intra- and inter-family level, and of course, the Family itself is always of great familial concern. Finally, the Government exists as everybody's favorite unindicted co-conspirator.

ANCESTORS: This topic enables us to keep old national stereotypes alive long after they've disappeared in Scandinavia. Example: "Well, I sure would have liked to have seen her this Christmas, but ever since she married into that Swedish bunch, you just can't count on her to keep any commitments . . ."

BREAKS: This is the Big One! It starts in childhood and lasts till they bury you. Then sometimes the kids take it up and it goes on for another generation or two. Basic form: "You always got The Breaks (from Mom and Dad, from teachers, from bosses, from life)! I had to *work* for everything I got!" Then you list *every* example you can remember where the other (usually a brother or sister) got a Break, particularly if you thought that Break came at your expense.

CHURCH: Don't expect a rousing argument on comparative theology when everyone in the house is Lutheran. But while no one may care to argue with you about the meaning of God's existence, you *can* get the whole crew yelling at once simply by talking about the manner in which God's church on earth is—or should be—run. Lutherans are not abstract theologians. We only go to confirmation once, but we go to *church* every Sunday. Doctrines come and go, but we know *church* backwards and forwards and will argue endlessly about anything to do with *church.* Why do you think we have so many synods?

DOMESTIC: While Scandinavian/Americans have never judged a woman strictly on her housekeeping, one of the oddest sights in nature is to watch a feminist daughter frantically dusting inaccessible places before her mother and all the female relatives show up for Thanksgiving.

Since all mothers believe that their children are perfect (the more the child resembles them, the more perfect they are), Domestic arguments tend to center on that perfect child's fall from grace—a fall usually attributed to her/his unfortunate choice of a spouse.

Daughter-in-law example: "If she didn't have my son to do all her housework for her, their house would be a wreck all the time!"

Son-in-law example: "I taught my daughter how to be a good housekeeper, and you know very well how spotless her apartment was before those two got married! But nobody can keep a house clean the way *he* continually clutters it up!"

EXPENSES: The taboo against talking about your income is so strong that a Scandinavian/American family would rather have you talk about sexual dysfunctions during Easter brunch than to have you give the details of your paycheck—anywhere, anytime. The only specific dollar amounts which may ever be politely mentioned in a Scandinavian/American family are: 1) the price of farm land, 2) the price of your new car, and 3) the sale price of any genuine bargain.

Since we can't very well argue dollar amounts, we argue about each other's misplaced economic priorities. Example: "It seems to me that there are better ways to spend your money right now than to: A) buy a second car, B) take a trip, C) buy a VCR, or D) go out to eat all the time."

FAMILY: We love to criticize the way other people (especially our own kin) raise their children because it is a wonderfully indirect way of criticizing those people and their life-styles. Furthermore, with children there is always the hope that honest criticism will make them more like us and less like their parents.

Children's clothing, in particular, is a matter of the liveliest concern for adults who are otherwise totally unconcerned with fashion. This can even reveal a nasty streak of grandparental competition ("How come they never wear the clothes *I* buy for them?"). Inadequately laundered and/or frayed clothing is seen as a sure sign of parental neglect, if not actual abuse. Example: "Sometimes I swear that those two buy their children's clothes at Good Will just so they'll have more money to spend on their computers, or records, or whatever they do with it all!"

GOVERNMENT: Since Scandinavian/Americans tend to be middle-of-the-roaders politically as well as every other way, there usually aren't a lot of violent political discussions at family gatherings. Families tend to be pretty uniformly more-or -less Republican, or more-or-less Democrat. This is a cozy and unspoken situation where only a new in-law with a burning need to make his views known is in danger.

This vague uniformity tends to magnify any slight divergency, and more than one family gathering has been treated to the spectacle of two uncles with identical opinions, each screaming that the other is a dangerous extremist.

Farmer/Entrepreneur Wayne Jorgenson plants the grass for his new ski resort near Hector, Minnesota. Wayne claims it is the world's first ski resort built specially for people with inner ear problems.

"I've had that problem myself off and on for something like 20 years, so I know what it's like," he stated recently. "I figure since those people always feel like they're falling anyway, why waste expensive mountain real estate?"

The resort offers dancer's barres on the beginner's "slope," and a theme restaurant named The Stirrup, Anvil & Hammer.

The Politics of Snow:
Cross Country versus Downhill Skiing.

Skiing is a political act for Americans: Republicans and Conservatives identify themselves by skiing downhill, while Liberal Democrats are to be found cross-country skiing. Since Scandinavians of all political persuasions ski at every chance, and in every manner possible, this rule is less rigid for Scandinavian/Americans than for other Americans.

In America downhill skiing is the exclusive domain of private enterprise. Though the sport is crawling with would-be jet-setters, only those supported by a fifth-generation trust fund can hop a Concorde to indulge an off-season urge for one of Argentina's better slopes over the 4th of July weekend.

Like the remote castles of medieval robber-barons, the finest ski resorts are in isolated mountain passes where the populace is as white as the snow. These mountain hideaways, with their private lodges, exclusive restaurants and pricy little shops, are specifically designed to allow Yuppies, Yumpies, and Preppies an opportunity for serious alcohol abuse while surrounded by their own class, away from the scrutiny of downscale elements.

Activists see downhill skiing as an elitist sport, requiring skills honed since childhood in an atmosphere of undeserved leisure. The act of being effortlessly chairlifted to the top of a mountain is, they contend, a capitalist metaphor for the undeserved rise of the White-Anglo-Saxon-Protestant-Male-Executive/Exploiter-Class and its minority collaborators.

The feeling of illegitimate superiority engendered by standing atop a mountain is not enough for these people. They must also have the narcotic effect of speeding down a slippery slope, in what Marx has called "The Opiate of the Classes."

Cross-country skiing, on the other hand, is the world's only 100 percent politically correct sport. Cross-country skis are all union-made by Scandinavian workers who have a higher standard of living than most Americans, so neither the masses nor the resources of the the third world are being exploited.

Unlike downhill skiing, which requires a huge and prohibitively expensive wardrobe, you can go cross-country skiing in anything from coveralls to authentic Norwegian knickers and wool socks. If your ideology has a dress code, cross-country skiing will not violate it.

You do not need to travel great distances to rent an overpriced lodge to ski cross-country because of the ready availability of open-access/equal-opportunity/non-elitist locations like the city parks, the zoo, and other places owned and operated by the government for the common good.

Here the truly committed activist can escape the false values of the petit bourgeoisie and experience life at its most primal level. Unfortunately, the primal level generally includes rabid farm dogs and very sleazy teenage boys in rusted-out snowmobiles.

Conservative downhillers see cross-country skiing as a dangerous, if not openly treasonable, anti-business conspiracy. They see the sport crammed with low-lifes dependent on government-owned, quasi-socialist snow communes established on temporarily disused railroad right-of-ways illegally seized by the government from the free-enterprise system.

Most of the country dismisses such talk as merely another reactionary tirade and cross-country skiers wear these attacks as a badge of pride.

In truth, the most radical elements at both ends of the political spectrum have never enjoyed any sort of skiing. Those who have a tendency to stick their foot in their mouths every few minutes find it particularly painful when wearing skis, and nobody wants to fall down while carrying a bomb on the way to the abortion clinic or draft office.

THE GREAT '62 SCALES TAX REVOLT.

Tax reform is a hot issue nowadays, and the electorate, the media and politicians have focused on taxes as if they were the only problem on the economic scene. Tax plans, tax proposals, and tax alternatives have become the political equivalent of Cabbage Patch Dolls—ungainly, homely critters which one cannot simply acquire, but must formally adopt and promise to love beyond all reason.

Even the lunatic fringe has gravitated to tax protesting as an excuse to acquire and use more dynamite, machine guns and secret passwords. The public outrage over taxes has reached such celebrity status that it is certain to soon be enthroned on that pinnacle of public consciousness—a cover story in *People* magazine.

For Minnesotans however, tax protesting is an old and established way of life. As usual, Minnesota led the nation with the first major tax protest in modern times: "The Great Scales Tax Revolt" of 1962.

The protest was triggered by an obscure revenue proposal by Rep. John Lind, from the southern Minnesota town of Klossner, to raise badly needed revenues by taxing the sale of certain recreational equipment.

It was a simple enough proposal and deserved the solemn consideration of both the authorities and the public, but rumor flew faster than solid information, and soon the state was in functional anarchy.

Before the bill was even presented on the House floor, Lind's secretary, Charla Skogstad, a woman well known for her wit, joked at coffee break, "The fishermen of this state are going to be paying a Scales Tax pretty soon."

This bon mot was overheard by the legislative assistant to Daryl Thormondson, a nearly catatonic representative from up north, who was faced with his first serious re-election challenge since 1948.

Daryl's constituency viewed the right to hunt and fish as God's greatest gift, second only—maybe—to property rights. Semi-shrewd politician that he was, Daryl immediately realized that he could ride this issue to an easy re-election. It was made to order for him: It involved a maximum of emotion and a minimum of homework.

Even so, he had trouble getting the issue off the ground. His first press conference failed when no reporters showed up. Fourteen years in the House had left Daryl as nearly invisible as flesh and blood could be, or at least as invisible as a representative whose only reputation was based on his ability to sleep through committee meetings could be.

He finally attracted media attention by playing his old Hardanger fiddle outside Governor Andersen's weekly press conference. The departing photographers and reporters loved his well-honed backwoods image, and Daryl was soon in most of the state's daily papers. More important to Daryl, he was in *all* of the weekly papers in his own district.

But the notion of taxing fishermen was so explosive that no backwoods politico could master it or control it for his own limited ends. Within two months, Daryl had made more speeches than he had during his entire career, appearing before every sportsmens' club north of Hinkley. This only made matters worse, because Daryl's inability to get his facts straight, and his fondness for the cheap shot, soon removed the last elements of reality from the debate.

Rumors about what the Scales Tax Bill would actually tax, and how stiffly, were imaginative to the point of paranoia. Some predicted that every fish caught would be taxed by the inch and the species. Little bullheads would be taxed lightly, while record muskies would be prohibitively taxed.

Some said that it was a federal conspiracy to register all fishing tackle, and on that awful day when the Rooskies came marching down the fishing path, the only patriotic way of fishing would be to dynamite the lakes and scoop up whatever floated to the top. Other fishermen whispered—and only after the strictest assurances of anonymity—that it seemed odd how *some* people always considered explosives as their first solution to every problem.

There was a brief flurry of alarm centering around the rumor that it was the Fish *Weighing* Scales that were to be taxed, or worse, regulated and inspected for accuracy. That struck at the very heart of the Bill of Rights, smacking of government intervention into free speech, free initiative and the pursuit of happiness. It was also the only rumor too preposterous to be believed, even in the lunatic atmosphere surrounding this proposal.

The state's newspapers took predictable stands, angrily championing whatever they thought was their readers' opinion. The northern papers printed every negative comment they heard regarding the Scales Tax, regardless of its source. Meanwhile, the papers in the south were contemptuously viewing the whole affair as symptomatic of what they called "the north's blindly rebellious nature."

It was the newspapers, in fact, which led the personal attacks on the bill's hapless sponsor Rep. Lind, labeling him everything from an "enemy of wetlands," to a "sour old farmer whose only experience with fishing comes from snagging the mud-sucking catfish of the Cottonwood River to supplement his pathetic farm income, along with his more lucrative feeding at the public legislative trough."

By this time, both major parties had quietly looked over the revenue bill popularly known as the "Scales Tax Bill," and had realized that while the bill had some promise, it certainly wasn't worth the political fall-out that it would create. A secret meeting of both the House and Senate tax committees was held at Loretta's Tea Room in Minneapolis, and all agreed that the safest course would be to raise the taconite tax again, and appoint a Blue Ribbon Panel to study the possibility of a general sales tax.

When news of this secret meeting broke, the public reacted with unexpected enthusiasm. People were exhausted and ready to agree to any tax hike that didn't affect their hunting and fishing. Unfortunately, the machinery of the Blue Ribbon Panel had already been set in motion, and it was impossible to call it back, or even speed it up to take advantage of this unforeseen political consensus.

Minnesota didn't get a general sales tax for another five years, and when it did arrive it caused another major uproar because the voters had by then forgotten their emotions during the "Scales Tax" scare.

Rep. Lind, the sponsor of the original bill, was defeated that year for re-election. While Lind's constituents fished little and cared less, they were furious about his new notoriety. They did not want their representative making a scene about anything except low corn- and milk-price supports, and were certainly not about to re-elect someone who had had an Iron Ranger make a public fool out of him.

Rep. Thormondson was easily re-elected that year, but his sudden celebrity had convinced him that he was meant for greater things than some two-bit State-House seat. He resigned his seat to devote his energies to the U.S. House race. Since nobody could figure out what his campaign slogan, "Your Man For The Outdoors in Washington!" meant, Daryl slowly drifted toward the new issue of Indochina and Vietnam. Uncertain of how exactly to pronounce it, Daryl nevertheless felt himself an expert on it because it involved guns, taxes and emotion.

Daryl never even got close to landing his party's nomination that year and dropped out of politics altogether. Nobody has heard much from him since, although it is rumored that he moved to the deep south, where he was reported to have been involved in several business dealings of questionable legality. There have recently been rumors that he has become quite religious, and is planning a political come-back.

SCANDINAVIAN/AMERICAN GOTHIC: Famous Painting.
Pastel on Masonite, 1984. 7 1/2" x 7 3/8"
Private Collection

Probably the most popular piece of Scandinavian/American art that has neither a duck nor a sunset in it, *Scandinavian/American Gothic* perfectly captures the Nordic enthusiasm for nature and is considered the crowning work of the Hypothermic School of painting.

High Fashion Scandinavian/ American Suits:

Pants, Leisure, and Snowmobile.

Scandinavian/Americans do not think in terms of fashion because, by definition, fashion is a realm of escape and make-believe. We believe in neither.

You cannot accuse people who go to films like *Cries and Whispers* of having an escapist mentality. Scandinavian/ Americans do not want to have to *pretend* that they're warm when they put on a snowmobile suit. The only conceivable reason anyone would ever wear a snowmobile suit is that it is absolutely and inescapably *warm!* For once we're assured that we'll be warm, we can go outside in arctic conditions and frolic about till all our exposed body parts are frostbitten. We do that to prove that we're not trying to *escape* winter.

Scandinavian/American fashion consists of three suits: Pants, Leisure and Snowmobile.

Pantsuits cover about as much skin as a snowmobile suit, but the only insulation in them is the polyester fabric of which they are made. Scandinavian/American women wear them year around to church, work and shopping. In the winter, pantsuits can be worn underneath a snowmobile suit. No matter how sweaty you may get in the snowmobile suit, the pantsuit will not wrinkle. There's a positive side to everything.

Leisure suits are the male equivalent of pantsuits. Always made of polyester, these suits usually come in pale pastels reminiscent of 1950s bathroom tiles. I always half expect to see a set of three black plastic filigree fish with black plastic filigree bubbles coming out of their mouths on the backs of these suits, particularly the pale aquamarine ones. That would be perfect—sort of a Scandinavian/American equivalent to those gaudy embroidered jackets GI's brought back from Korea.

Finally, the snowmobile suit. The perfect Scandinavian/American *hot couture*. An insulated suit which does not breathe, for people who are out in the cold not exercising. With its nylon shell, it makes you look like a cross between a 1940s auto mechanic and a 21st-century android. Its main appeal is that it has no waist, and therefore does not embarrass you publicly.

I'd like to take a few minutes now to deal with the few fashion concerns Scandinavian/Americans do have, like how to wear your belt below your belly. I might even have some nice things to say about polyester and doubleknit. You never know.

The Wearing of the Belt.

Like everybody else, we Scandinavian/Americans don't dress to conceal ourselves. We use clothing to flaunt, expose or accent those body parts we most cherish.

Which is not to say that there are not genuine orthopedic fashions around—muumuus, pregnant-executive business suits, coveralls and parkas—but they all have either social or time limits.

An executive who wears her Brooks Brothers maternity suit for 11 or 12 months at a stretch will make her coworkers extremely uncomfortable. Similarly, anyone wearing that wonderful one-size-fits-all parka much past Syttendemai will make himself extremely uncomfortable. At some point dieting becomes the least painful alternative.

But most of us aren't ashamed of, nor even particularly unhappy with our bodies. Our attitude is: "It's mine, I've earned it and I'm going to flaunt it!" This is why the plunging beltline is so popular among Scandinavian/American Males.

The plunging beltline, like the plunging neckline, graphic-

ABOVE:
Wearing the belt below the belly.

RIGHT:
Wearing the belt above the belly.

Transpolar Navigation Lesson #1:
The shortest route between two
points is never along the equator.

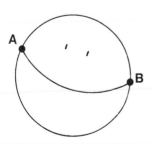

ally displays the body in all its sensuous splendor. Sweeping lines plunge down to affirm that symbol of nourishment—the full belly. Accented by an ostentatious belt buckle, the plunging beltline is one of Scandinavian/American males' two favorite fashions.

The other is the soaring beltline.

Known also as the Nordic empire waistline or the timberline waist, this is a favorite among more mature gentlemen with full-sized stomachs. Instead of plunging below the belly, the timberline waist soars triumphantly above the navel, coming to rest safely atop the belly plateau, free of any tug of gravity.

Even with the baggy pants favored by these elderly gentlemen,the inseam always seems to be pulled awfully tight. But maybe after a certain age, things like that aren't as critical.

The tummy-top belt-line also means that the pants legs are pulled far enough up to reveal ankle-length black socks, always with clocks, and a bit of that delicate old-man skin the color of Lutefisk.

What I learned from the young uncles with their plunging beltlines and belt buckles large enough to knock out a yearling calf, and from the old uncles with their high beltlines, grey slacks and stomachs that looked like lunar globes, was Trans-Polar Navigation.

I learned that the shortest beltline between two points is not directly along the stomach's equator: The shortest route is to go over (or under) the pole.

There is no way to answer those benighted souls who huff that these men should just buy larger trousers and fix their pants the way they *ought* to be. That's nothing but appeasement, and will only get you into deeper trouble. Stomachs expand to fill the waistline available to them, and that's an historical fact!

There's nothing wrong with a "full-figured stomach." We all ought to remember that St. Olaf (before he became posthumously known as Olaf the Holy), was known to all his Viking pals as Olaf the Fat.

And who says there are no good Nordic Role Models?

POLYESTER:
THE CURSE OF THE MIDDLE-AGED.

This business of being snide about polyester has gotten out of hand recently. Artificial fiber seems to bring out artificial humor. Both have limited aesthetic appeal.

We've all heard the glee with which certain people reported the accident in a boiler room aboard a Navy ship a few years back. The seamen, dressed in natural fibers, were scalded by the steam, to be sure, but the officers, dressed in their new polyester uniforms, were killed when the uniforms melted and intensified their burns.

But that's not the point. The point is that if they *had* survived, they would have looked much less rumpled than the seamen did as they ran out of the room screaming, "That Blinkety-Blankety thing is leaking steam again!"

Let the preppies have their all-natural fibers. The last time they were in a boiler room was when they volunteered to staff the phone banks for the George Bush campaign. It's fun to look delightfully tousled and rumpled only when you don't have to work for a living.

If your job description involves more than networking and conceptualizing, you want *un*rumpled clothing to disguise the fact that you are working like a dog.

If you're not a perfect size three (or a man with a 32 inch waist), you want clothing that doesn't wilt along with you as the day progresses, leaving you at 5 p.m. looking like a steamed dumpling served in sweat sauce.

Scandinavian/Americans' fashion demands have always been simple and straightforward. All we want is something which, 1) looks OK, and 2) doesn't rip or rumple.

We're not the sort of people who demand ever-newer fashions to express our personalities. We do not enjoy expressing our fashion sense any more than we enjoy expressing any other personal opinion in public.

Allow me to share some common Scandinavian/American fashion criteria:

Polyester Positives:

Designer jeans don't come in polyester.

Polyester clothes don't have someone else's name on them.

They're cheaper, because there's always a good selection left during the close-out sales.

You can lose up to five pounds a day in water weight alone from July through mid-September by wearing a three-piece polyester suit with a polyester shirt and tie.

You look better in polyester at a distance than you do close-up. And what Scandinavian/American wants to get too close?

Polyester clothes do not rip in embarrassing places when you stoop, squat, reach, bend or leap.

Polyester offers you the smug, politically correct assurance that your vanity is exploiting no Third World animals, worms or labor.

Doubleknit is an inherently moral and modest fabric. For example: No one has ever staged a wet doubleknit-pantsuit competition.

The Down-Side of Doubleknit:

If you lean against a stucco wall while wearing doubleknit, you may not be able to leave when you want.

By sagging in odd spots, doubleknit manages to draw attention to bodily features you had hoped to hide.

You cannot dry your hands by wiping them on your clothes, because polyester absorbs *nothing.*

Your fear of public speaking is probably justified while wearing polyester/doubleknit. Many audiences have been heard to snigger openly when a person in polyester comes to the podium.

Your clothing may melt if left in the back window of your car.

Polyester tends to glisten and glimmer in certain lights. This is acutely embarrassing to many Scandinavian/Americans, who feel that if they had wanted to look like Michael Jackson, they would have bought sequins in the first place.

While your lap may disappear when you stand up, the baggy spots around your knees remain visible for some time.

Your clothes never wear out, and you cannot even get rid of them by pouring grape juice on them, because the damned stain always washes out.

FIRE AND ICE:

Scandinavian/American Sex Amid the Wind-Chill.

Scandinavian/Americans are plagued with contradictory stereotypes. On the one hand, Nordics are supposed to be as sexy as all-get-out. On the other, we're known to be Lutherans.

Americans are all familiar with the evils of Scandinavian Pornography (Known hereinafter as "SCANDPORN"). Lurid and silly films like *Sexual Freedom in Denmark* or *I am Curious, Yellow* have played to packed houses of gawking, scratching Americans. For all the supposed sophistication of American audiences, we are rubes and suckers for anything with a bunch of women running around bare-nekked.

To live up to our sexy stereotype, we Scandinavian/Americans would have to wear nothing but polyester tigerskin briefs and garter belts from Fredrick's of Hollywood.

But if we're so sexy and sensual, how do you account for all those orthopedic undies—you know, the white cotton kind a quarter of an inch thick, that pull up nearly halfway to milady's armpits? Real-life Scandinavian/American women buy their undergarments from Fredrickson's of Sioux Falls, not from Fredrick's of Hollywood.

Fredrickson's has a complete line of "See-Through Down-Filled Intimates." Camisoles with both eye appeal and R-value. They're guaranteed to keep you warm till that perfect partner comes along. This blending of eroticism and practicality is what has given Scandinavian/Americans their reputation for sexual ingenuity. Something has to keep us warm up here!

No-Waist Nudes:
When will America rebel against the No-Waist/No-Romance
ideology?

NO-WAIST NUDES:
The Sculptures of Vigeland.

If Scandinavians are universally thought of as a sexy bunch, it's because they do not restrict sexuality to beach bunnies and Nautilus freaks. Nowhere is this democratization of passion more obvious than in Vigeland Park in Oslo.

Here, one is surrounded by hundreds of sculptures of 'full-figured' nudity: men and women of all ages, triumphantly flaunting cellulite thighs, waists that match the hips inch for inch, and figures that in America would be shrouded in muumuus and polyester golf shirts.

These are figures whose idea of exercise is to go to an afternoon movie, and who can laugh off indigestion by smothering it with more chocolate cake. But in America, figures like these are seen as asexual, so large that they can reproduce only by splitting apart.

Is it any wonder, then, that America looks to Scandinavia for erotic liberation? On a pure percentage basis, more of us look like Vigeland's sculptures than like Bo Derek. And we aren't about to let the Bo Dereks of the world have *all* the fun!

In Vigeland's sculptures, I see and recognize human shapes I have known and loved. Loved repeatedly and compulsively, I might add. Even though Vigeland's intention in creating these sculptures was not erotic, it is refreshing and energizing to see their substantial flesh imbued with such energy. People without waists should not be without hope for romance.

Postal-Orgasmic Sex.

Non-Scandinavians seldom realize that those bright red POST boxes in front of Scandinavian/American homes are not simply theft-prone receptacles for mail.

They are actually a secret sign denoting that a person or persons of a wildly passionate nature live at that address.

To understand the full erotic significance of these attractive, conspicuous devices, you must delve into our Scandinavian heritage.

The postal services of the Scandinavian countries have a centuries-old tradition of extreme efficiency. Mail arrives so quickly, and with such personal service, that it has been possible for years to have an affair entirely by mail in Scandinavia.

Singles bars, museum openings, and Luther League dances have almost entirely disappeared in Scandinavia as the need to personally meet new people of the opposite sex has dwindled.

In fact, postal sex has entirely replaced confrontational sex for many Scandinavians because it is tidier, makes fewer demands on the emotions, and doesn't turn your face and chest all splotchy red.

While the U.S. Postal Service is not efficient enough to allow correspondents to carry on a conversation, let alone a romance, many Scandinavian/Americans still display their bright red POST boxes to make a subtle yet colorful statement about their private lives.

But like all Scandinavian/American communication, it's a hint inside a nuance inside a suggestion, and it's up to you to figure out what it means.

The Secret Language of Purses.

Lutheran college women (being Scandinavian/American) believe in communication by osmosis, if at all. This means that Lutheran college men get very few clues about how any given date will turn out.

Scandinavian/American women do not hint that it's going to be a hot date by showing up in a Harley-Davidson tube top and a vinyl miniskirt. On the other hand, they don't bring little battery-operated cattle prods to let you know they'd rather be washing their hair. But over the years, a system has evolved for rating the evening's romantic prospects. It's all in the bag. Or bags, in this case.

Briefly stated, the larger the purse, the duller the evening. The smaller the purse, the more amusing the night. The further away the purse is placed, the more interested your date.

It's simple logic and logistics. A purse the size of a hockey equipment bag, jammed emphatically between you and your date, might as well be the continental divide. No romance for you unless you're Jeremiah Johnson.

A medium-sized purse, placed carefully on her lap, is an ambiguous statement: You, and the "relationship," are still on probation. One of those little purses that would fit inside a business envelope, tossed casually over by her door, isn't going to hinder anything, nor is it meant to.

So you see, there *is* communication, even innuendo, among Scandinavian/Americans. The photo chart below shows the subtlety of expression possible with only three representative purses and three basic positions.

If you are dating, or considering dating a Lutheran, this chart will help you communicate with, and perhaps even somewhat understand your partner. You might even grow to enjoy this sort of game. Generations of Lutheran college students have certainly learned to love it.

"The Continental Divide"

CONTENTS:

A week's worth of books, plus at least one extra pair of clogs. Has to be checked at airports. Also comes in the shape of a backpack and/or an athletic bag.

"The Am-bag-uity"

CONTENTS:
Could contain a toothbrush and a change of clothes, but doesn't. Instead, contains 3 lipsticks, a chapstick, 7 pencils, a pack of gum, 1 cloth glove, $12.17 in change and a paperback romance.

"Just the Essentials"

CONTENTS:
Small perfume bottle, Bianca, *Purple Rain* tape, toothbrush, and several things that are none of your business.

"The Continental Divide"
in Action.

"Forget it!"

"You'd have to lift this thing off my lap before you even thought of getting romantic, and let's face it—Arnold Schwarzenegger you ain't."

"I can still cave your head in with this thing if you push me too hard.'

"The Am-bag-uity"
in Action.

"Kerstin told me all about your date with her last week..."

"...but I think she's a little too proper for her own good..."

"...and besides, she just doesn't know how to deal with someone as cute as you are..."

"Just the Essentials"
in Action.

"Well, hello…"

"How do you get these ideas?"

"Where?"

The Nuclear Family Reaches Meltdown:

Family Reunions as Critical Mass.

We are living in sentimental times, and our leaders court ruin if they dare say that there are problems in the American family. But as one with no electoral ambitions, I can tell you the truth. And the hard truth is that families can make you crazy!

The nuclear family fuels an endless chain reaction of hassles, problems, irritations, and dilemmas. A substantial number of people would rather go skinny-dipping in the Three-Mile Island cooling tank than dive into a "family holiday."

Thanksgiving, Christmas and Easter are family days in America, and Scandinavian/Americans are not alone in occasionally dreading them. We are strong people, with strong wills, and it can be a mighty test of those wills to throw together relatives who no longer have anything in common.

We don't outright *fight* when we get together. We're like lawyers intent on discovery: We spend our time gathering evidence to use against each other for years to come.

"Did you hear what Arne said about Grandpa's boat?" someone will ask. Resist the temptation to reply, "Why didn't you bring it up to him right there?" It's obvious they enjoy having the huff-puffs about it. By the next family get-together, they will have called or written everybody (except Arne) about it, and forced everyone to choose a side.

In the final analysis, it isn't love that keeps us coming back to family gatherings (although it exists more tenaciously than it

has any reason to). We return because all these people know the background of all the arguments, and they know the *correct* way to fight them. They may not always fight fair, but they fight *familiar*, and that's the next best thing to being loved.

Arguing Politics with a Deaf Uncle.

No Scandinavian/American family gathering is complete without a good, surly political "discussion." These are not discussions in the usual sense, where certain people are trying to change other people's opinions about a given topic. Scandinavian/Americans do not come to family gatherings to have their brains slipcovered. They come to say things that need saying.

Nor do these discussions follow some abstract debating protocol—1st affirmative followed by 1st negative, on down to rebuttals and closing statements. Since everyone knows beforehand what everyone else will say, the pattern is closer to that of a play (except that everyone is reading from a different script)

The Sandvik Family Greets Their New Baby in Chinese.

For reasons that are still unclear to modern science, most Scandinavian/Americans (like most Americans) instinctively speak to their newborns in Chinese.

Try to remember how frightening it was to be a baby. You're 20 inches tall and weigh about 9 pounds. You're quietly lying there in your crib doing aerobics with your toes, when suddenly you're surrounded by these 6-foot, 200-pound barbarians bellowing what sounds like Chinese at you — "Ah Goo, Coot-Chee-Coo!"

What a terror and confusion that must be for babies. Why don't we speak English to them? They won't understand it any better, but they'll have more use in later life for English than Chinese.

Or is this just some genetic residual from our distant ancestor, the Peking Man?

than a true debate. Besides, during a formal debate, everybody isn't allowed to yell at the same time.

Family political discussions are largely responsible for the stoic nature of Scandinavian/Americans. Young people first enter these discussions full of passion and idealism, but a few short years of arguing with deaf uncles takes a lot out of a person. It makes you realize that sincerity is a fuel, not a solution. It makes you vaguely suspect of all enthusiasms, beginning with other people's and extending eventually to your own.

And it reminds you that other people didn't ask your permission to form their opinions, and probably won't drop them to suit you either.

Who are the players in this great family dialectic? They're not hard to identify for they're always the same people, arguing about the same things they always argue about. Here's one family's worth:

Great-Uncle Olin: Believes that public morality began its decline when electricity replaced the wood stove. Easy electrical living, according to Olin, is the devil's playground. Youngsters who once had—literally—to "keep the homefires burning" had no time for mischief, and developed sound limbs, clear lungs, thrifty and industrious habits, and a patriotic outlook.

Aunt Beverly: Suspects a media conspiracy is afoot because none of her three letters to the editor of the Renville County Journal about the health dangers of spitting in public has ever been published.

Aunt Elaine: Attends all high school plays in a three-county area with a notebook and a penlight to document any use of "those words." Takes bashful credit for having been instrumental in the forced resignations of two teachers and an assistant pastor.

Uncle Keith: Still proud of having cast his first ballot for the socialist Norman Thomas in 1940. His early radicalism has mellowed into a moderate Republicanism, but he remains suspect to family ideologues on both sides.

Uncle Howard: Only his legendary inertia keeps him from becoming a full-fledged survivalist. His life is so slow-paced that he could be called laid-back, if only he weren't always angry about something.

Aunt Doris: Still nursing a grudge because her brother Tom was sent to college in 1925 and she wasn't. Her malapropisms (You've got to take anything he says with a grain of truth.") are a major source of comic relief, although no one is allowed to laugh while she's still in the room.

Uncle Carl: Extremely proud of his title as the family conservative. His car (American-made, of course) is covered with angry bumper stickers. He can be counted on for impromptu half-hour harangues on treason, trilateralism, and biblical prophecies. Sports is the only topic that he can't turn into a political monologue. People talk a *lot* of sports with him.

Aunt Kay: Loves the excitement of a good argument and will take any stand to provoke one. Then she stands back and watches the fireworks.

Cousin Maren: The family's only out-and-out feminist, she is also the only one besides Uncle Carl who still puts her money where her mouth is. She is a lawyer and is active in nine women's groups ranging from a rape crisis center to a women's theatre/poetry collective.

Uncle Carl suggests that she is gay because she supports the ordination of women, and anti-family because she helped set up a battered-women's shelter.

Cousin Paul: Although he likes to describe himself as an "activist with roots all the way back to the Yippies," Paul's only known confrontation came when he designed a "No Quisling Zone" poster with a swastika inside the red circle with a slash. By displaying this piece of prop art when Uncle Carl came for Thanksgiving, he nearly split the family in two.

Paul no longer takes an active role in politics, having convinced himself that his major contribution to changing the world lies in arguing with his unchangeable relatives.

Civic Pride In Whatever:
The District IV, Winneshiek County Pork Queen and Her Parade.

One of the little drawbacks in living close to the land is that other folks may not necessarily appreciate the same things you do. The Blackduck FFA Honors List, for example, seldom makes the CBS Evening News. Which is a shame, really, because a good group of Future Farmers is going to be more useful than most of the other things that have to be reported every night.

Rural Scandinavian/Americans love a parade in the next town because it's a great excuse for the whole family to come to town together, see friends and have a look at the shops. Merchants like parades for the same reason.

It may be hard for big-city folks to understand why the local news photographer needs three motorized, 60-frame-per-second cameras to cover a parade like this.

It is probably also hard for big-city folks to understand the enthusiasm that young women might feel for a Pork Queen competition. It doesn't seem like the sort of thing one would put on a resume, or even use as a stepping stone towards the Miss America pageant.

But it's probably a hotly contested title. Starting at the local level, there are Pork Queen auditions, contests and rehearsals. Essays on "Pork and the American Way of Life" weed out the intellectually slothful and the inappropriately sardonic.

So give Ms. Schutte and the photographer their due. She is an attractive young woman who is learning about irony in a very personal way, and doing so with all the dignity and good humor she can muster. The photographer is playing it straight, photographing her in as regal a setting as a small town provides. She is not posed with two scrubbed piglets and a half unbuttoned calico blouse. She is losing only the dignity we fail to extend to her.

Besides, what beauty competition has any more dignity than a Pork Queen Contest?

Playing it straight at Decorah's Nordic Fest, complete with a convertible and three motorized Nikons.

Little Secrets in the Bookshelf.

Just as a tree can be dated by reading its rings, you can tell a Scandinavian/American's age by counting the number of *Lutheran Hymnal* revisions and back issues of *National Geographic* magazine with articles about Scandinavia in their bookshelves.

How can you identify a true Scandinavian/American bookshelf?

It's easy if there is a Dala horse, a little Nordic flag (or flags), or a rosemaled doo-dad on top. Otherwise, you have to check out the contents.

It's a Scandinavian/American Bookshelf if it contains at least One (1) Book from Column A and Two (2) Books from Column B.

COLUMN A	COLUMN B
Markings, by Dag Hammarskjold	*Of Swedish Ways*
Living God's Way, by Reuben Youngdahl	*Of Norwegian Ways*
Kon Tiki, by Thor Heyerdahl	*Of Danish Ways*
A Collection of either Ibsen's or Strindberg's plays	*Of Finnish Ways*
Anything by Kierkegaard	Any big, dull, four-color picture book about Scandinavia
Ingmar Bergman's Screenplays	*Pippi Longstocking,* by Astrid Lindgren
	A six-year-old program from Svenskarnasdag

WEATHER OR NOT:

"And the Coldest Spot in the Nation Today IS. . ."

L et's face it. Minnesotans think the whole rest of the country, including Iowa, is a bunch of wimps when it comes to weather. Nothing amuses us more than listening to Dan Rather say "Dallas, Texas, was shut down today when the worst winter storm of the season dumped 2/325 of an inch of snow on the Dallas area." But when they turn the cameras on Mrs. Bettybob Leubadeubadeux as she sobs, "Ma Gawd, we jest cain't get nowhere! Mah husband, Billybob IV, like-unto *ruined* his snakeskin Gucci loafers trying to get to the office this morning. . . ," that's when Minnesotans realize what superior folks our winters have made us.

It doesn't take many Minnesota winters to develop a Nordic stoicism about weather. Whatever minor psychological price this may entail, it certainly is better for both the individual and the group than the Sunbelt self-pities or the Western whines.

We're proud to come from a state that regularly has the coldest morning temperature in the lower 48 states. It's good, cheap PR. And because we love our weather, we wear it with style. We're colder than Scandinavia? So what? Who cares if Buffalo, N.Y., gets more snow? We get the winter sports people. Michigan a winter wonderland? Not unless you want to cross-country ski across miles of unsold automobiles.

But mostly we love our Arctic playground because it enables us to exercise our Nordic attributes: sullen depression, cabin fever and repressed hysteria. What more could you ask from nature?

Like reading the rings of a tree trunk, scientists can tell a Scandinavian/American's age by the number of Lutheran Hymnal revisions and National Geographics in his/her bookshelf.

Traveler's Advisories.

When the weathercasters on the radio or TV announce "There are traveler's advisories out for tonight," most of us simply assume that they are referring strictly to meteorological conditions that would make driving unpleasant. We assume that's just a formal way of saying, "Hey folks, it's sleeting out there, and 35W has just entered the *Guinness Book of World Records* as the world's longest iceskating rink."

But Scandinavian/Americans have always known that there are worse things than a little snow on the road. We are very familiar with a little snow on the road. It's those little surprises that have to do with *people* which can ruin a trip for us. That's the sort of danger which traveler's advisories are intended to warn us about.

Like all Scandinavian/American communication, traveler's advisories are indirect and implied. You are expected to know beforehand what they are talking about, or at least be able to figure it out for yourself.

So when the radio says: "Traveler's advisories are out for all of southern Minnesota," here's the sort of subtext that's important.

- Travelers are advised that the Sportsman's Grill in Blue Earth is now charging extra for coffee refills.

- Travelers are advised to watch out for Connie Huseboe, who waitresses at The Cat'N'The Fiddle Restaurant just outside Hanska. Connie has been known to get her orders mixed up, and sometimes doesn't add up the tab just right either.

- Smart-aleck travelers from the Twin Cities are advised not to make fun of the phrase "Soup du Jour of the Day" on the Menu at the Dew-Drop-Inn in Bird Island. Hostess Lucy Setteruud put that phrase in there herself so people would at least know what they were ordering. Lucy has always felt that people who want to speak a foreign language when they're eating would be better off in a big city like Minneapolis or Sioux Falls, rather than out bothering people who have to work for a living.

- Holidays or not, travelers are advised *never* to put a French silk pie, or any cream pie, in the rear window. You'll ruin your entire trip and make yourself a nervous wreck worrying about having to stop suddenly and maybe getting whipped cream all over the back seat or the back of your neck.

- Those traveling with children are advised to keep them physically separated by obeying the seatbelt laws, and are further advised that they can stop that annoying bickering by spraying the kids' gums with an aerosol dental anesthetic, available from better dental supply houses.

- While it's certainly annoying to have to stop constantly for potty breaks for your children, travelers are not advised to scare them before leaving home with the graphic details of an unscheduled potty break on the prairie with a windchill of -40. That sort of thing is often considered child abuse, and can lead to agoraphobia later in your children's lives.

- Those traveling through the western suburbs of Minneapolis in tacky cars, pickups with big wheels and jacked-up suspensions, or vans with scenes painted on their sides are advised to expect sniggers from the locals.

- Status-conscious travelers are advised to avoid Nordeast Minneapolis, where a BMW is only another foreign car.

- Travelers are advised to bring an adequate supply of their own audio tapes, since no station in southern Minnesota is going to match their musical tastes—no matter what those tastes are.

- Travelers are advised that The Red Carpet Motel just past Fulda has changed management, and no longer seeks the patronage of those folks who do not register in their own names.

- Travelers who do not register in their own names are further advised that Denise, who used to work at the Standard Station next to The Red Carpet Motel, has recently gotten married and moved to Georgia.

- Anyone planning to travel in this kind of weather is advised to reconsider their motives. Why are they going? What do they hope to accomplish? Are they driven by guilt to visit relatives whom they despise? Do they expect large gifts in return at Christmas? Wouldn't it be easier and safer to take care of business by phone? What are they trying to get away from?

- Out-of-State Travelers should remember that all roads in Minnesota

IS SNOW TOXIC?

Despite incontrovertible and mounting evidence of such afflictions as snow-blindness, frost-bite and hypothermia, no government agency has dared to come to grips with the basic health question facing Minnesotans: Is snow toxic?

are North-South roads. What appear to be East-West roads are only East-West segments of North-South roads. The only exception to this rule is the federally mandated Interstate 90 in southern Minnesota, which was supposed to be built in northern Iowa.

Our road system was planned in this way to facilitate the mass exodus of Minnesotans to Upnorth, the generic name for any place with cooler weather when summer forces the cool air out of most of Minnesota. It was also intended to keep businesses from moving to South Dakota for tax write-offs.

- There are only two travel seasons in Minnesota: Winter and Under Construction. "Good Winter Driving Conditions" means that you will not spin out on ice until you have nearly arrived at your destination.

"Good Summer Driving Conditions" means that you cannot

In this hithertobefore unpublished photograph, we see actual Minnesotans overcome by snow toxicity. A crisis of this magnitude must be addressed by a combined effort of the Center for Disease Control and the Environmental Protection Agency! Write to your Congressional representative today and demand that something be done!

reach your destination directly because all the roads in the county are under construction. The roads are not actually closed as they usually are in winter, so you *can* travel them, but only at 7 MPH (4.2 KmPH).

The Minnesota Children's History Museum now offers a *Travelfun Packet for Kids* entitled "How Your Ancestors Traveled by Oxcart, and Why They Couldn't Stand to Go Any Further."

With highway crews preventing you from traveling any faster than your immigrant ancestors did in oxcarts, the kids can play games where they imagine having to travel another month at this pace to reach South Dakota's lower corporate taxes. Most kids choose to stay where ever they are at that very moment than go on—just like their ancestors.

THE WINE-CHILL FACTOR:
(A.K.A. The Wind-Chill Factor).

Contrary to popular belief, the wind chill factor was not discovered by a Scandinavian. It was discovered in 1908 by a Preppy, Morton J. Throckmorton, who had been thrown out of Princeton University for "Habitual tardiness and stuff."

What actually happened, was that while attempting to return to college after one of his monumental binges in Philadelphia, Mr. Throckmorton had staggered onto a train, handed the conductor a wad of bills and demanded to be taken to Princeton.

Unfortunately, he had mistakenly boarded a westbound train, and slept all the way to Minneapolis. At the Princeton, Minn. depot he staggered off and, incapable of any further exertion, decided to stay.

It was January and, ever the perceptive Gentleman/ Scientist, Throckmorton noticed that he was less comfortable when the wind was blowing. He also noticed that the bottles of wine left outside in the wind and snow cooled faster than the bottles left in a protected place in the snow. (He also noticed that bottles left in the sun cooled more slowly than shaded bottles. Had he stayed sober, he could have discovered solar heating as well.)

Thrilled to make this discovery of the wine chill effect, Throckmorton attempted to patent his discovery and start an exporting firm based on its principles. Fine wine could be shipped to Minnesota, where it would be chilled. He would then ship it back East in sealed cars, assuring himself a fortune to drink up in the future.

The business suffered a setback, however, when his family had him placed under the legal guardianship of the law firm of Throckmorton, Throckmorton and Throckmorton. His patent application was never filed, and eventually passed into the hands of the Minnesota Historical Society's Humor Archives.

Sloppily made out and full of misspellings, the application caught the eye of Carl Isbjorn in 1962. Carl, a WCCO Radio weathercaster, corrected what he thought were spelling errors and fine-tuned the meteorological details.

He also tried to patent it under the name of Carl's Coldness Chart. The name never caught on, and the patent was later refused on the grounds that no one should benefit from making other folks feel even more miserable than they already do during a Minnesota winter.

ONE-, TWO-, AND THREE-OBSCENITY COLDS.

We each have our own private way of organizing the world into a system we understand. These personal perceptions of natural phenomena get sorted out till they fit into a master plan, that helps us come to peace with the world around us.

On a grand scale, this leads to such philosophical peaks as Lutheranism, Epicureanism, and the notion that rock and roll records can be played backwards to reveal hidden messages. On a more practical scale, Scandinavian/Americans have converted this quest for meaning and order in life into a pragmatic search for realistic ways of coping with winter.

I've studied some other people's systems, and frankly, they leave me baffled. For example: I can find no useful reason why I should have to come to grips with, or even comprehend, a ski wax chart.

It's all so complicated: "At -10 to -35 degrees Farenheit (-21 to -34 degrees Celsius) below an altitude of 6,654 ft. (2055 meters), use blue/green wax, unless you have oak/cedar/redwood laminated skis, when you would use the yellow/orange wax, unless the snow is unusually sticky, or white, or compacted, or the wind velocity is between 15 and 40 MPH (24 to 64 KmPH), and your weight, including skis, pack, parka and too much wine in that ridiculous frat-boy wineskin you still carry around, is between 150 and 175 lbs."

Whenever I stare—blankly—at one of those posters with its 50 or so mini-commandments, I never understand why it simply doesn't say: "At -10 to -35 degrees Farenheit (or Celsius—at that temperature, it doesn't make any difference), you'd have to be compulsive to go outside. Go home and take a nap—you need to catch up on your sleep."

My system for coping with winter is far more direct. As a writer, I deal with winter by throwing words at it—words which I hope will hurt it as much as it hurts me. They never do, of course, but at least I get the smug feeling that somehow I've made my contribution to the solution.

All cold is divided into three parts: One-obscenity cold, two-obscenity cold, and three-obscenity cold. Unlike psychoanalysis, which claims that the act of describing a fear is the first step in banishing it, my system acknowledges that your fear of cold is probably well-founded.

In other words, it's still going to be cold after you've cussed your lungs out at it, and, depending on how long you've been cussing, it will probably have turned even colder than it was when you began.

There is a fourth category, probably not as rare as we would like, in which the ritual act of cussing reaches such momentum that the sufferer cusses with an eloquence and passion powerful enough to fuse the torrent of language into a glistening whole, awing and inspiring even the stray foreigner, who cannot understand a single word but can perfectly comprehend the emotional sincerity of the performance.

If you ever find yourself in a situation where you feel called upon to engage in such oratory, remember to avoid obscenities with sibilant vowels, such as "s"—particularly if you lisp. Park rangers often find cussers who are spitters frozen to their ski poles, still sputtering like an old outboard motor inside a solid shell of ice.

A final note of warning: If you ever come across someone who is not cussing in the cold, don't commend them on their virtue. Seek medical help for them at once, because they're already at the point where they're probably seeing bright lights and long-departed relatives welcoming them to warmer climes.

ONE OBSCENITY COLD	TWO OBSCENITY COLD	THREE OBSCENITY COLD
– – – –, it's cold!	– – – –, it's colder than a – – – –!	Oh – – – –, it's so – – – – cold that I'm going to – – – – freeze to death!
Your breath condensation freezes in your mustache.	Your breath condensation freezes your entire beard.	Your beard freezes right down to the skin.
Clenched teeth.	Clenched buttocks.	Clenched pores.
Snow bunnies.	Grizzly bears.	Polar bears.
The garden hose you left out freezes.	Your car radiator freezes.	Your bathroom pipes freeze.
You keep warm by vigorous cross-country skiing, carrying a little wineskin.	You keep warm by relaxing in front of a roaring fire, sipping on hot drinks.	You try to keep warm by wrapping yourself in a blanket in front of a roaring fire and gulping aquavit—straight.
Romantic moonlight walks listening to the snow crunch beneath your feet.	Brisk daytime hikes between your car and the grocery store, listening to the ice crack on the lake.	No unnecessary travel at all, listening to the radio tell how many seconds unprotected skin will endure before the onset of terminal frostbite.
Perpetual sniffles.	Hacking cough.	Pneumonia.
The Snow Queen by Walt Disney.	Any Hemingway story.	*To Light a Fire,* by Jack London.

BERGMANIA:
Depression as Intellectual Chic.

Ingmar Bergman is the cultural savior of Scandinavian/ Americans. We share in his reflected cultural glory like poor relatives, and our fellow (non-Scandinavian) Americans think of his films as documentaries of our lives. It stands to reason: They understand neither Bergman's films nor us, and neither we nor his characters ever say much or show any particular emotion.

Despite his alleged retirement, Bergman remains a major cultural force in film. At parties, people will still spot your blond hair, walk across the room, poke you in the chest and say something like "Ah betchew laik Bergman, huh?"

As before, the more cultured ones will walk up and, without introducing themselves, say, "I've always personally enjoyed his chamber films, but my husband, who likes his pleasures somewhat more direct, prefers the allegorical period, with the exception of *The Virgin Spring*, of course."

And there you are. Stuck for an appropriate response. All your Ole and Lena jokes and all your torsk recipes count for nothing here. They don't want to hear about that part of your heritage. They want to hear about Bergman! From a Scandinavian! Someone who *instinctively* knows about depression, the si-

---

The officers of The Seventh Seal Fan Club (Naima Wifstrand chapter) pose for their formal portrait at the club's annual meeting in Tofte, Minn. Left to Right: Ron Wahlstrom, Vice President; Laura Nyberg, Treasurer; Ardys Kvilhaug, President; and Bonnie Eyrich, Secretary.

lence of God, and the other zany elements of Bergman's films. What these people actually are trying to do is to prove that they know more about being Nordic than you do because they know their Bergman so well. Don't let them.

Bergman discussions are exercises in One-Upsmanship. One-Upsmanship is a game where two or more people try to pull intellectual rank on each other. As games go, it's not much fun, but it does have its joys for the sedentary and the idly vicious.

In the typical discussion, you're pitted against people with varying degrees of expertise on Bergman. Don't worry about that. Excess knowledge only slows down the intellect. Besides, you're the Nordic, and what is Bergman but the Great Nordic?

It is often easier to defeat an expert than a dilettante. The true Bergmaniac must be intimate with Bergman films most people haven't even heard of. Experts haven't the luxury of simply saying that they've never heard of such and such film. An unseen film is a dangerous chink in their armor.

Even if your idea of culture is a banquet at the Sons of Norway lodge, you can One-Up college professors when it comes to Bergman. Just follow these rules.

Faking Your Way Through Ingmar Bergman.

1. Use only the Swedish titles to the films. Your opponent likely will know more than you do about *Winter Light,* but if you start talking about *Nattvardsgästerna,* he/she will hesitate and lose momentum.

   Then try reciting your grandmother's table prayer with great feeling, and pass it off as film dialogue. You can draw any conclusion you want, and use any set of Scandinavian phrases as proof. The rules of evidence do not apply here.

2. Use appropriate language. If you enjoy talking like Sylvester Stallone, you would be well advised to limit your film criticism to the *Rocky* films.

   Example: "That was a dumb movie" is not acceptable criticism once you have left grade school. To have your criticism heard and registered in a serious film discussion, trying saying things like "That film lacked the coherency and insights one expects of even a *National Enquirer* article . . ." Remember that film buffs do not care *what* you think as much as *why* you think it and *how* you express it.

3. Never sound like you've actually completed a sentence. Always let your voice trail off, as if to say, "But that's so complicated I don't want to get into it right now . . ."

4. Never go willingly to a dubbed film—always go to subtitled films. If nothing else, this proves you are literate, an increasing rarity among American filmgoers.

5. Never laugh or react at the same time as the rest of the audience. If you don't speak Swedish, learn to speed read subtitles so it appears that you are fluent in Swedish and thus receiving untold subtleties unavailable to monolingual Americans.

6. Discover what your opponent *doesn't* know and use that against him/her. The true Bergmaniac would prefer to lose the occasional argument rather than admit ignorance.

7. Never budge an inch on the supremacy of Bergman. Give only the faintest praise to all other directors, and then only in the ways in which they resemble Bergman. Make it clear that you consider them lesser lights and copycats.

8. Read every review and book on Bergman you can get your hands on. They are an invaluable source of "personal" insights and observations. If their writers seem to have seen and heard things you missed, it doesn't mean you weren't paying attention. It only shows you how much livelier their imaginations are.

9. Always stay for the credits, and make a comment about something obscure. (Warning: "Hey, we visited there!" is not an appropriate comment. Bergman's films are set in the mind—not in Värmland. If you *must* show your friends where you have traveled, you would be well advised to stick to home, Gidget, and cowboy movies.)

10. If—despite everything—you are losing a Bergman discussion, simply say "Well, that's a uniquely Swedish (or Nordic) concept, and it's hard to translate to Americans with the sort of consumeristic pop-culture we're drowning in."

Then refuse to discuss it any further, and change the topic, preferably to something like how Gjetost cheese is made, or Volvo engineering standards, to show your mastery of Scandinavian ways.

Keeping Score in Bergmanical One-Upsmanship.

One-Upsmanship is a game, and therefore must have clear-cut ways of scoring points. Otherwise, film parties would have nothing to talk about except who was sleeping with whom. There are two general rules for scoring Bergman One-Upsmanship contests, and an all-purpose scoring chart.

1. No points are given for any Bergman film seen in a shopping mall or in a multiple screen theatre.
2. Films are rated according to their inaccessibility and obscurity. Recent films (anything since *Cries and Whispers*) get no points, except *From the Life of the Marionettes*, which no one saw anyway.

Scoring Chart:

+12 every book of Bergman criticism you own, written in Swedish.

+10 every 30 minutes of coherent, nonrepetitive discussion of *Persona*.

+10 every Bergman film you saw in Sweden during its first run.

+9 every Bergman film you saw in Sweden in re-release.

+9 making your own translation of a Bergman screenplay from the French, as it appeared in *Cahiers du Cinema*.

+7 making your own translation from a Bergman screenplay from the Swedish original.

+6 leading a discussion, with examples, of Bergman's debt to Swedish silent-film directors.

+5 all Bergman films before *The Seventh Seal*.

+3 all Bergman films made between *The Seventh Seal* and *Persona*.

+3 just seeing *Persona*. Never mind understanding it.

+1 all Bergman films made after *Persona*.

+3 each personal, sentimental reminiscence of *Fanny and Alexander's* Swedish Christmas scene.

+4 if you get teary reminiscing about the Christmas scene.

+3 each film you identify exclusively by its Swedish title.

+2 each film you identify exclusively by its British title.

+1 for identifying every motif (over five) in *Fanny and Alexander* which first appeared in another Bergman film.

−3 every dubbed film you've attended.

−5 analyzing Bergman's films for political content.

−5 saying that you don't like Bergman because you can't understand him, without explaining why you feel that way.

−10 going to a Bergman film for the nudity.

CRIES AND MUTTERS:
The Ultimate Bergman Trivia Quiz

A trivia quiz about Bergman may seem like a contradiction in terms. Nothing about Bergman is trivial. It is hard to imagine a man who makes films about death and the silence of God doing folksy things like eating cold soup out of a can, or vegging out in front of the TV after a hard day's work at the philosophy phactory.

The man *does* have a private life, but a combination of Nordic privacy and a profound distaste for gossip columns makes him keep his private life as private as is possible for a cultural celebrity.

Even Bergman fanatics often know very little about their hero's life. Bergman himself has told a few stories about his childhood (which may or may not have been improved upon for dramatic impact), and there are recurring motifs in his work which everyone assumes are personal references. While there has never been a dearth of academic articles in which scholars presumed to read Bergman's mind to the rest of us, only recently, has an English-language biography of Ingmar Bergman been published: Peter Cowie's wonderful *Ingmar Bergman: A Critical Biography*. Many of the personal tidbits about Bergman were gleaned from this book, so all you compulsives who can't stand to be beaten in trivia games can read the book before you take this quiz.

1. What were the names of Bergman's parents?
   A. Andreas and Thea Bergman (nee Winkleman)
   B. Erick and Karen Bergman
   C. Johan Bergman and Alma Borg
2. What was Bergman's birth order?
   A. Only child
   B. Youngest child
   C. Middle child
   D. Oldest child
3. Bergman's grandmother had a huge apartment where he spent much of his time as a child, and which figured prominently in many of his later films. Where was that apartment located?

    A. Stockholm
    B. Berlin
    C. Uppsala
    D. Oslo

4. Bergman's father was employed as a:
    A. Professor of Antiquities
    B. Medical Doctor
    C. Civil Servant
    D. Lutheran Minister

5. In 1934, during his youth, Bergman was sent to a foreign country on an exchange program, heard a political leader speak and for the only time in his life took an active interest in politics. What country, what leader and what movement?
    A. He went to Russia, lived with a family whose children were all Young Pioneers, heard Stalin speak, and returned to Sweden as a "pro-Soviet fanatic," as he later described himself.
    B. He went to Palestine, lived with an Israeli family on one of the first kibbutzim, heard Ben-Gurion speak, and returned to Sweden as a "pro-Zionist fanatic," as he later described himself.
    C. He went to Germany, lived with a family whose children were all Hitler Jugend or Hitler Mädchen, heard Hitler speak, and returned to Sweden as a "pro-German fanatic," as he later described himself.
    D. He went to Louisiana, worked in a CCC camp, heard Huey "Kingfish" Long speak, and returned to Sweden as a "good-ole-boy populist, but still a fanatic," as he later described himself.

6. In 1942, while directing a play at the Student Theatre, Bergman was called out and given his first job at Svensk Filmindustri by Stina Bergman, widow of the great Swedish writer Hjalmar Bergman (no relation). What job was he given?
    A. Researcher
    B. Screenwriting assistant
    C. Designer
    D. Director

7. Bergman's first script to be filmed was:
    A. *Torment*
    B. *Crisis*
    C. *It Rains on Our Love*

8. Bergman's directing debut was a film called:
    A. *Torment*
    B. *Crisis*
    C. *It Rains on Our Love*

9. Bergman started wearing a beret in 1943. Why?
    A. His first wife, the dancer Else Fisher, wore one, and he adopted it as a badge of artistic courage.
    B. His father delivered a sermon attacking them, causing Bergman to buy one and wear it to church next Sunday.
    C. His politics having shifted radically in the past nine years, he

adopted the beret as a symbol of the French resistance to Nazism to berate the "pathetic neutrality" of Sweden during the war.

10. When a production of *The Ghost Sonata* was cancelled after three performances, Bergman blew up at an actor (who would figure prominently in his later films), because the actor demanded to be paid for the full run, claiming "I have to eat!" (To which Bergman is said to have replied "Food! Who in hell says you've a right to food? Live on coffee and cookies like me!")
    A. Stig Olin
    B. Anders Ek
    C. Gunnar Björnstrand

11. David O. Selznik of Hollywood paid Bergman 30,000 kroner in 1948 for writing a screenplay for a movie that was never produced. What movie?
    A. *An Enemy of the People*
    B. *A Doll's House*
    C. *The Dance of Death*

12. Bergman once said, "Only once has it happened that I've made something I've known from the beginning would be rubbish." What film was he describing?
    A. *High Tension*
    B. *Music in Darkness*
    C. *Three Strange Loves*

13. In 1951, Bergman made nine commercials to help pay his bills. What was the product?
    A. Sjöstugarna: a resort developer in Småland
    B. BRIS: the first deodorant soap in Sweden
    C. Volvo: for its first commercials shown in the U.S.

14. What film had to be largely reshot because the negative was so badly scratched by the processor?
    A. *The Seventh Seal*
    B. *The Touch*
    C. *Monika*

15. Who was the only person during the shooting of *The Naked Night* to be able to make friends with the thoroughly ill-tempered bear in the circus?
    A. Harriet Andersson
    B. Ingmar Bergman
    C. Gudrun Brost

16. Bergman often signs his scripts with the initials "S.D.G." just as Johan Sebastian Bach did at the end of every composition. What do those initials mean?
    A. *Soli Deo Gloria*—"To God alone, the glory."
    B. *Summus Delecti Gnosis*—"This is the delight of wisdom"
    C. *Sich Dar'f Guttesmachen*—"This is good work"

17. What Bergman film was a spy-thriller about the Cold War?
    A. *High Tension*

    B. *Prison*
    C. *Port of Call*

18. How many times did Bergman rewrite *The Seventh Seal* screenplay?
    A. He rewrote it seven times, thus giving it its name.
    B. The first script was letter perfect, allowing for some minor improvisations in certain scenes.
    C. He rewrote it five times

19. What play is *The Seventh Seal* loosely based on?
    A. *To Damascus,* by August Strindberg
    B. *Painting on Wood,* by Ingmar Bergman
    C. *Easter,* by August Strindberg

20. Which Bergman film had so many special effects that special effects pipes had to be imported from all over Scandinavia?
    A. *Fanny and Alexander*
    B. *Hour of the Wolf*
    C. *The Magic Flute*

21. How long did it take to film *The Seventh Seal?*
    A. 35 days
    B. 124 days
    C. 259 days

22. Where were the location shots done for *The Seventh Seal?*
    A. Heimaey, in Iceland
    B. Hovs Hallar, in Skåne
    C. Tromsø, in Norway

23. What Bergman film is rebroadcast annually at Christmas time throughout Europe?
    A. *The Seventh Seal*
    B. *Autumn Sonata*
    C. *Fårö-document*
    D. *The Magic Flute*
    E. *Monika*

24. In 1948, a young unknown actor telephoned Bergman while he was preparing *Prison,* and asked for a chance to audition for a bit part. Bergman simply cut him off. Who was that actor?
    A. Marlon Brando
    B. Max von Sydow
    C. Klaus Kinski

25. At the Mälmo Theatre in the late '50's, Bergman put up a sign board during rehearsals with a phrase written in 97 languages. What was that phrase?
    A. "Precision!"
    B. "Restrain the Character!"
    C. "Shut Up!"

26. One of Bergman's greatest actresses was married to a film critic who regularly used to savage Bergman. Bergman initially cast her in a film

hoping—successfully—to neutralize her husband's criticism. Who was she?
- A. Ingrid Thulin
- B. Gunnel Broström
- C. Bibi Andersson

27. What characters were described as having "one of the few happy marriages in Bergman's world"?
- A. Katarina and Peter Egerman, in *From the Life of the Marionettes*
- B. Stina and Harry Andersson, in *Brink of Life*
- C. Anne and Henrik Egerman, in *Smiles of a Summer Night*

28. Which of Bergman's wives was born on the same day—14 July—that he was?
- A. Käbi Laretei
- B. Gun Grut
- C. Ellen Lundström

29. What was Bergman's first film shot in color?
- A. *The Passion of Anna*
- B. *The Devil's Eye*
- C. *All These Women*

30. In 1972, Bergman's brother Dag was appointed Swedish ambassador to what country?
- A. France
- B. USA
- C. USSR
- D. Greece

31. Which of the five senses is hypersensitive in Bergman?
- A. Sight
- B. Smell
- C. Touch
- D. Taste
- E. Hearing

32. What film was originally to be titled *Cinematography?*
- A. *Face to Face*
- B. *Scenes From a Marriage*
- C. *Persona*

33. What was Bergman's first dramatic film to be shot in color?
- A. *The Passion of Anna*
- B. *Stimulantia*
- C. *Scenes From a Marriage*
- D. *From the Life of the Marionettes*

34. Bergman is reputed to have asked what famous actress to star in *The Silence?*
- A. Grace Kelly
- B. Marilyn Monroe
- C. Greta Garbo
- D. Audrey Hepburn

35. Which of these film(s) have/has won an Academy Award(s)?
    A. *The Virgin Spring*
    B. *Through the Glass Darkly*
    C. *Cries and Whispers*
    D. *Fanny and Alexander*

36. Which Bergman film grew out of Bartok's description of his *Concerto for Orchestra:* "The dull continuous note, and then the sudden explosion"?
    A. *The Silence*
    B. *Winter Light*
    C. *Shame*

37. Which Bergman film has 60 speaking parts and 1,200 extras?
    A. *The Serpent's Egg*
    B. *Fanny and Alexander*
    C. *The Magic Flute*
    D. *Smiles of a Summer Night*

38. Bergman chose women for the technical crew when filming *Autumn Sonata* because he said "they were more efficient and less hysterical than men." What percentage of that crew was female?
    A. 20%
    B. 50%
    C. 66%
    D. 100%

39. What Bergman film about art and movie critics did Bergman call "an outburst of really bad temper"?
    A. *Torment*
    B. *All These Women*
    C. *The Magician*

40. Which Bergman film had its American premiere in a New York theatre (The Rialto) known for its striptease movies.
    A. *Monika*
    B. *All These Women*
    C. *The Silence*

41. Which of his films did Bergman describe as "a lousy imitation of Kurosawa"?
    A. *Hour of the Wolf*
    B. *Virgin Spring*
    C. *The Devil's Eye*

42. In 1963, Bergman directed the European continental debut of what play?
    A. *Long Day's Journey into Night*
    B. *Who's Afraid of Virginia Woolf?*
    C. *A Man for All Seasons*

43. What film was cancelled because Bergman fell seriously ill?
    A. *Hedda Gabler*
    B. *The Cannibals*
    C. *Gisli's Saga*

44. During the filming of what movie did Bergman first discover his beloved island of Fårö?
 A. *Monika*
 B. *Scenes from a Marriage*
 C. *Through a Glass Darkly*

45. *Scenes From a Marriage* was originally filmed to run as six TV shows of 48.5 minutes each. How long was the theatrical-release version?
 A. 4 Hours, 51 Minutes
 B. 4 Hours, 15 Minutes
 C. 3 Hours, 31 Minutes
 D. 2 Hours, 48 Minutes

46. In what three films does Max von Sydow play Bergman's alter ego in claustrophobic island settings?
 A. *Hour of the Wolf*
 B. *Brink of Life*
 C. *The Passion of Anna*
 D. *Fårö-document*
 E. *Cries and Whispers*
 F. *Shame*

47. Bergman lives on an island which is off-limits to foreigners because it is a top-secret military radar installation. True or False?
 A. True
 B. False
 C. How did you obtain this information, and from whom?

48. What type of car is Bergman's favorite at his home on Fårö?
 A. A '58 Chevy
 B. A Peugot
 C. A Volvo that he gets free—yearly—from Volvo, AB
 D. An antique Rolls Royce

49. Where did Bergman spend his childhood summers?
 A. Stockholm
 B. Dalarna
 C. Germany
 D. Lappland

50. During the filming of which film did the lingering summery weather force the actors and crew to climb trees to pick the fall leaves off one by one, so as to achieve the proper tone of desolation for the film?
 A. *Hour of the Wolf*
 B. *Virgin Spring*
 C. *The Passion of Anna*
 D. *Shame*

51. During the filming of which film did an early summer force the film crew to keep moving farther and farther north to maintain a supply of trees whose leaves were just beginning to bud?
 A. *Hour of the Wolf*
 B. *Virgin Spring*

C. *The Passion of Anna*
D. *Shame*

52. What was Liv Ullmann's first film with Bergman?
A. *The Devil's Eye*
B. *Face to Face*
C. *Persona*

53. In *The Magician*, the suave, cynical scientist Dr. Vergerius loses to Bergman's alter ego—Albert Vogler. In what film does a similar Dr. Vergerius defeat the chief characters?
A. *The Serpent's Egg*
B. *From The Life of The Marionettes*
C. *Shame*

54. In 1968, Bergman established a company named after Louis Lumiere's early motion-picture machine. What was the name of the machine, and the company?
A. Heliograph
B. Biopticon
C. Cinematograph
D. Realigraph

55. What film did Bergman shoot in nine days, and cast himself in the role of priest/confessor?
A. *Stimulantia*
B. *The Rite*
C. *Fårö-document*

56. In 1969, Katherine Ross and Viveca Lindfors were scheduled to star in a film which was never shot. This film was to have been co-directed by Bergman and what other director?
A. Jan Troell
B. John Huston
C. Federico Fellini
D. Jean-Luc Goddard

57. Many of Bergman's screenplays have sprung from plays he wrote previously, but what screenplay was later turned into a play and performed as one third of a triptych along with *A Doll's House* and *Miss Julie?*
A. *Scenes from a Marriage*
B. *Secrets of Women*
C. *All These Women*
D. *A Lesson in Love*

58. What film was set in an exact replica of the Uppsala apartment owned by Bergman's grandmother?
A. *Fanny and Alexander*
B. *Face to Face*
C. *Wild Strawberries*

59. Of what film did Bergman's wife say, "Yes, Ingmar, it's a masterpiece; but it's a dreary masterpiece."
A. *Winter Light*

B. *Persona*
C. *The Seventh Seal*

60. Bergman pays homage to Fritz Lang in *The Serpent's Egg* by having his character, Inspector Bauer, call on Lang's character, Inspector Lohman, for a professional chat. Who is the model for Inspector Bauer?
   A. The Swedish tax official who arrested Bergman
   B. The head of the Swedish Tax Office
   C. The Swedish Prime Minister
   D. Bergman's Swedish tax lawyer

61. Why did the Savoy Grill in London refuse to serve Bergman in 1969?
   A. Because he was not wearing a tie
   B. Because he was living out-of-wedlock with Liv Ullmann
   C. Because he had recently punched a prominent British critic

62. What film drew its actors from Munich's Residenzteater Company?
   A. *The Serpent's Egg*
   B. *Illicit Interlude*
   C. *From the Life of the Marionettes*
   D. *Music in Darkness*

63. Who was the first English-speaking actor/actress in a Bergman film?
   A. Karen Landry
   B. Elliott Gould
   C. Clyde Lund
   D. Adaire Petersson

64. In what film did he/she appear?
   A. *Autumn Sonata*
   B. *The Touch*
   C. *Summer Interlude*
   D. *Thirst*

65. In the incomprehensible world of Timoka in *The Silence,* as the sisters grapple with language they cannot speak, what is the only comprehensible word in the newspaper?
   A. J.S.Bach
   B. Death
   C. Invasion
   D. Fascism

66. What Bergman film features three actresses, each evoking separate aspects of his mother's personality?
   A. *Secrets of Women*
   B. *Cries and Whispers*
   C. *Persona*
   D. *Shame*

67. What film about a couple did Bergman describe thusly: "They are alone, and the world is coming to an end."
   A. *Hour of the Wolf*
   B. *Shame*
   C. *The Passion of Anna*

68. Which of these Bergman players has also directed a movie which Bergman produced?
A. Gunnel Lindblom
B. Max von Sydow
C. Liv Ullmann
D. Gunnar Björnstrand

69. In 1972, Bergman announced he was planning to film the light operetta *The Merry Widow*. Although it was never filmed, who was scheduled to star in it?
A. Julie Andrews
B. Koo Stark
C. Barbra Streisand
D. Audrey Hepburn

70. What Guthrie alumnis played the Gunnar Björnstrand role in *A Little Night Music*, Broadway's tribute to Bergman's *Smiles of a Summer Night*?
A. Paul Ballentyne
B. Peter Michael Goetz
C. Ken Ruta
D. Len Cariou

71. What film is set in a country whose language is completely unintelligible?
A. *Shame*
B. *The Silence*
C. All those Swedish films

72. In Bergman's play *Painting on Wood*, the Knight is mute. Why?
A. Bergman was responding with pique to criticism that his work was "overly literary."
B. All the characters were mute. The play was a mime set to Carl Orff's *Carmina Burana*
C. The part was originally written for a handsome actor who couldn't deliver serious dialogue

73. What Bergman film was shot and distributed in English?
A. *The Touch*
B. *Scenes from a Marriage*
C. *The Rite*
D. *Face to Face*

74. Where was the first major filmography and study of Bergman's career published?
A. France
B. England
C. Sweden
D. Uruguay

75. In 1972, Bergman wrote one of three screenplays for a film that was never produced. Who was to write the other two screenplays?
A. Frances Ford Coppola
B. Federico Fellini

C. Mike Nichols
D. Richard Attenborough

76. What was Bergman's first film shot in Germany?
A. *From the Life of the Marionettes*
B. *The Serpent's Egg*
C. *Fanny and Alexander*

77. Bergman has said, "_____ actors still represent the sort of theatre I love most of all: robust, direct, concrete, substantial, sensual."
A. Nordic
B. Commedia Del Arte
C. Musical comedy
D. Medieval

78. Of which city did Bergman say: "_____ exerted an almost demonic suggestiveness over me—_____ wasn't the real _____ at all, but a city of black destruction."
A. Berlin
B. Moscow
C. Washington, D.C.
D. Hollywood

79. What film was produced as a response to a friend who asked if Bergman "so obviously loved life and found parts of it so amusing, why did [he] consistently produce gloomy and depressing movies?"
A. *The Magic Flute*
B. *All These Women*
C. *Fanny and Alexander*
D. *The Devil's Eye*

80. Which film had 3,000 extras?
A. *The Serpent's Egg*
B. *The Seventh Seal*
C. *Fanny and Alexander*
D. *Fårö-document*

81. What film has been described as "a detective story without a solution"?
A. *The Serpent's Egg*
B. *The Passion of Anna*
C. *The Touch*

82. Bergman felt that *The Passion of Anna* was a second attempt to tell a story he had failed to tell to his satisfaction in what other movie?
A. *The Touch*
B. *Shame*
C. *The Silence*
D. *Persona*

83. *Autumn Sonata* was originally to be filmed in English. Who insisted that it be filmed in Swedish to reach a larger audience?
A. Ingrid Bergman
B. Ingmar Bergman
C. Liv Ullmann

D. Dino De Laurentis

84. What film is set somewhere in occupied Eastern Europe?
    A. *Ship to India*
    B. *The Silence*
    C. *High Tension*

85. How many children does Bergman have by his various wives?
    A. 2
    B. 4
    C. 8
    D. 14

86. *Scenes from a Marriage* features an acidic party with two couples—the film's main characters (Johan and Marianne) and a bitterly unhappy couple (Peter and Katarina). In what other Bergman film do the characters Peter and Katarina appear as a couple?
    A. *From the Life of the Marionettes*
    B. *Cries and Whispers*
    C. *Divorced*
    D. *Frenzy*

87. Which Bergman play was presented in the United States in 1972 on TV's Playhouse 90, subtitled for Americans: "A tragic comedy about banality"?
    A. *From the Life of the Marionettes*
    B. *Face to Face*
    C. *Scenes from a Marriage*
    D. *The Lie*

88. In 1980, Bergman was appointed president of the Cannes Film Festival to restore the honor and integrity the awards had lost. When he resigned, unable to effect his suggested reforms, who replaced him?
    A. Jean-Luc Goddard
    B. Charlton Heston
    C. Kirk Douglas
    D. Michelangelo Antonioni

89. While *Winter Light* and *Shame* had disappointing premiere showings, one of Bergman's films ran to an average of only 64 people per theatre during its Swedish first run. Which film was that?
    A. *From the Life of the Marionettes*
    B. *The Seventh Seal*
    C. *The Silence*
    D. *The Naked Night*

90. What film featured home movies of Bergman's son?
    A. *Persona*
    B. *Stimulantia*
    C. *The Silence*

91. Inspired by hearing Stravinski's *A Psalm Sunday* on the radio, Bergman set out to make a film about "a solitary church on the plains of Uppland." When his retired minister father furiously marched up to

take over the pathetic service led by a bored and incompetent minister for a nonexistent congregation, Bergman realized that he had the core of what film?
A. *Through a Glass Darkly*
B. *Winter Light*
C. *The Silence*

92. Dustin Hoffman, Al Pacino, George Segal, George Harris, David Carradine and Max von Sydow were all considered for what role?
A. David Kovac, in *The Touch*
B. Peter Egerman, in *From the Life of the Marionettes*
C. Johan, in *Scenes from a Marriage*
D. Abel, in *The Serpent's Egg*

93. At what temperature does Bergman keep his sound stages, considering it the ideal temperature for technicians and actors alike to work in.
A. 64
B. 70
C. 76
D. 84

94. In Bergman's "last film," *Fanny and Alexander,* it was widely assumed that Bergman's alter ego was the young Alexander. But Bergman has refuted this idea, suggesting another character whom he feels represents his personality more fully. Who is this character?
A. Bishop Edvard Vergerus
B. Oscar Ekdahl, the father who dies of a heart attack
C. Isak Jacobi, the antiques dealer
D. Carl Ekdahl, Alexander's farting, drunken uncle

95. Bergman has said: "The people in my films are exactly like myself—creatures of instinct, of rather poor intellectual capacity, who at best only think while they're talking. They're mostly body, with a little hollow for the soul." Given all that, what TV show does Bergman claim to watch regularly, taking delight in the fact, that as he says, "It's so bad it's good!"
A. "The Benny Hill Show"
B. "Jerry Falwell's Old Time Gospel Hour"
C. "Lifestyles of the Rich and Famous"
D. "Dallas"

96. Bergman has been married or "romantically involved" with which of these women?
A. Else Fisher
B. Ellen Lundström
C. Gun Grut
D. Käbi Laretei
E. Ingrid Karlebo
F. Harriet Andersson
G. Liv Ullmann
H. Malin Ek
I. Nancy Reagan

97. Which of Bergman's wives gave up the title of countess to marry Bergman?
A. Käbi Laretei
B. Ingrid Karlebo
C. Gun Grut

98. What childhood nickname did Ingmar's family know him by?
A. *Mörker Mats*—"Gloomy Gus"
B. *Tokig*—"Nutsy"
C. *Putte*—"Little Chap"

99. In which of these films has Ingmar Bergman appeared?
A. *Thirst*
B. *To Joy*
C. *Secrets of Women*
D. *Viking Women and The Sea-Serpent*
E. *Dreams*
F. *The Rite*

100. What actor has appeared in the most Bergman films?
A. Max von Sydow
B. Gunnar Björnstrand
C. Birger Malmsten
D. Gösta Pruzelius

101. What actress has appeared in the most Bergman films?
A. Bibi Andersson
B. Harriet Andersson
C. Liv Ullmann
D. Ingrid Thulin

102. Who has appeared in the most Bergman films?
A. Birger Malmsten
B. Bibi Andersson
C. Gunnar Björnstrand
D. Harriet Andersson

103. What actor was in both Bergman's first film and his last film?
A. Erland Josephson
B. Gunnar Björnstrand
C. Allan Edwall
D. Gösta Pruzelius

104. What actress was in both Bergman's first film and his last film?
A. Harriet Andersson
B. Gunn Wållgren
C. Maud Hyttenberg
D. Svea Holst

105. What two actors have been with Bergman since his second picture through to his last film?
A. Gösta Pruzelius
B. Allan Edwall
C. Jarl Kulle

D. Erland Josephson

106. Much is made of Bergman's "repertory company" of actors. How many people have acted in more than eight of his 43 films?
   A. 3
   B. 9
   C. 14
   D. 29

107. Who is the only actress to make a movie with both Ingmar Bergman and Bob Hope?
   A. Signe Hasso
   B. Maud Hyttenberg
   C. Anita Björk
   D. Renee Björling

108. *The Silence* is set in Timoka, a city of unexplained and vague dangers. The name comes from a book of Estonian poetry that belonged to one of Bergman's wives. What does Timoka mean in English?
   A. The Judge
   B. The Hangman
   C. The Anarchist
   D. The Affair

109. What film sprang from Bergman's vision of "a large red room, with three women in white whispering together?"
   A. *Cries and Whispers*
   B. *Waiting Women*
   C. *The Pleasure Garden*
   D. *All These Women*

110. Bergman's wife Käbi Laretei was a world class concert pianist who introduced Bergman to Stravinsky and other great composers. How did she describe their evenings together?
   A. Private chamber orchestra performances which Bergman joined while playing a bronze-age flute
   B. Calm evenings where she read aloud to him, concentrating on Russian literature (especially Chekhov's short stories) and musical biography
   C. Calm evenings where she read aloud to him, concentrating on Swedish literature (especially Strindberg's short stories) and Hans Christian Andersen
   D. Large parties of intellectuals and artists, where everybody outdid each other to perform or exhibit some new work of art or theory

111. Bergman started wearing a beret in 1943 after seeing one on his first wife. Does he still wear one?
   A. No. He saw a critic he despised wearing a beret, and he never wore one again
   B. No. His fourth wife put a stop to that
   C. Yes. But only to tweak the Swedish concept of the well-dressed-man

112. Which of Bergman's wives were dancers?

A. Else Fisher
B. Ellen Lundström
C Käbi Laretei
D. Gun Grut

113. Which of Bergman's wives was a journalist and a specialist in Serbo-Croatian history and current affairs?
A. Käbi Laretei
B. Ellen Lundström
C. Else Fisher
D. Gun Grut

114. Which Bergman film was based on an old Swedish folk song, called *Töre of Vänge's Daughter?*
A. *Hour of the Wolf*
B. *The Magician*
C. *The Virgin Spring*
D. *A Lesson in Love*

115. What film led to speculation that its real subject was "The atmosphere of persecution and psychological sadism that was engendered by the [tax] authorities in Sweden?"
A. *The Silence*
B. *Prison*
C. *Torment*
D. *The Serpent's Egg*

116. If *Fanny and Alexander* was billed as "Bergman's last film," how do you account for *After the Rehearsal?*
A. It was actually filmed before *Fanny and Alexander*
B. *After the Rehearsal* was intended only for TV, and released in America to theatres against Bergman's wishes
C. Even Bergman can't afford to retire, Swedish taxes being what they are

117. Georg Buchner once said: "Man is an abyss, and I turn giddy when I look down into it." Which of Bergman's films did that quotation inspire?
A. *The Serpent's Egg*
B. *The Devil's Wanton*
C. *Crisis*
D. All of them

118. Which Bergman film has been described as a "French sex-farce filtered through Nordic mysticism."
A. *It Rains on Our Love*
B. *Last Couple Out*
C. *The Magician*

119. Which film was considered so shocking that Bergman and his wife received several death threats?
A. *The Silence*
B. *The Devil's Wanton*
C. *Night is my Future*

120. What three Bergman films feature three women in restricted settings and their relationships to their emotionally distant husbands?
A. *So Close to Life*
B. *Journey into Autumn*
C. *Secrets of Women*
D. *Cries and Whispers*
E. *The Land of Desire*

121. Which Bergman film was considered responsible for a further jump in Scandinavian divorce statistics when it was shown for the first time on TV?
A. *Divorced*
B. *Scenes from a Marriage*
C. *Summer Interlude*

122. *Gycklarnas Afton* was released in America under the lurid title *The Naked Night*, although Britain more sensibly titled it *Sawdust and Tinsel* to reflect its circus setting. What would be the best title for this fine film?
A. *Illicit Interlude*
B. *Sawdust and Tinsel*
C. *A Bunch of Nasty, Heathen Swedes Running Around without a Stitch of Clothing!*
D. *Night of the Jugglers*

123. What film has ungenerously been called "A film a man would make in lieu of going mad"?
A. *Torment*
B. *While the City Sleeps*
C. *Hour of the Wolf*

124. Fairly early in his career, Bergman directed a film scripted by someone else to deal with "abortion and the obligations of a social-welfare system." While this is the sort of *cinema verite* which Scandinavian/Americans absolutely refuse to attend, it's really a pretty good film. What title is it used in its rare American showings?
A. *The Pleasure Garden*
B. *This Doesn't Happen Here*
C. *Three Strange Loves*
D. *Port of Call*

125. Even though Bergman's wife Gun Grut developed the concept and assisted Bergman in writing the screenplay for this picture, and even though Bergman insisted that she receive a credit line in the film for her contributions, Svensk Filmindustri refused the credit line because they felt that the movie-going public "needed convincing that Bergman himself could write a smart, witty film." Which smart, witty film was it that treated Ms Grut so badly?
A. *Secrets of Women*
B. *To Joy*
C. *A Lesson in Love*

126. What was the only Bergman movie to premiere outside Sweden?

A. *Fanny and Alexander*
B. *From the Life of the Marionettes*
C. *The Serpent's Egg*
D. *The Touch*

127. Which of Sweden's greatest directors from silent film days did Bergman convince to act in one of his early films?
A. Mauritz Stiller
B. Victor Sjöström
C. J.W.Brunius

128. The Knight plays chess with Death in *The Seventh Seal*. What does the Knight play with Death in the wonderful parody of Bergman films, *De Duve?*
A. A duet with spoons and harmonica
B. "Starlight, Starbright..."
C. Racquet ball
D. Badminton

129. Bergman seldom uses amateur actors in his films, but he did once, with excellent results, in *Journey into Autumn*. Who was the actor?
A. Marie Gotobed (French tourist)
B. Elsa Hansson (nanny to Bergman's children)
C. Kerstin Hedeby (production designer)
D. Sune Olafs (Bergman's tax probation officer)

130. Bergman once offered Liv Ullmann the female lead in his upcoming movie. She wearily turned it down because she was "tired of all that doom and gloom." What movie was that?
A. *The Ritual*
B. *Smiles of a Summer Night*
C. *Summer Interlude*
D. *Fanny and Alexander*

SCORING FOR BERGMAN TRIVIA QUIZ

1.B	20.C	39.B	58.B	77.D	96.All but I	115.D
2.C	21.A	40.C	59.A	78.A	97.B	116.B
3.C	22.B	41.B	60.D	79.C	98.C	117.A
4.D	23.D	42.B	61.A	80.A	99.All but D	118.C
5.C	24.B	43.B	62.C	81.B	100.B	119.A
6.B	25.C	44.C	63.B	82.B	101.A	120.A,C,D
7.A	26.A	45.D	64.B	83.A	102.C	121.B
8.B	27.B	46.A,C,F	65.A	84.B	103.B	122.D
9.A	28.A	47.A	66.B	85.C	104.D	123.C
10.C	29.C	48.B	67.B	86.A	105.A,D	124.D
11.B	30.D	49.B	68.A	87.D	106.C	125.A
12.A	31.E	50.D	69.C	88.C	107.A	126.C
13.B	32.C	51.B	70.D	89.A	108.B	127.B
14.C	33.A	52.C	71.B	90.B	109.A	128.D
15.A	34.C	53.A	72.C	91.B	110.B	129.C
16.A	35.All	54.C	73.A	92.D	111.B	130.D
17.A	36.A	55.B	74.D	93.A	112.A,B	
18.C	37.B	56.C	75.B,C	94.A	113.D	
19.B	38.C	57.A	76.B	95.D	114.C	

Tack så Mycket!

There are so many people who need to be thanked for their help, encouragement, and occasional honest criticism in the development of this book that I would have to devote half the book's space to do them justice.

Special thanks are due to the models in these pictures. They are too numerous to name, they all know who they are, and a couple are already wondering what appearing in this book will do to their careers. I would like to apologize to any members of the Peterson, Oas, and Anderson families whom I missed photographing for this book. They'll have to appear in the next book.

I am very grateful for the help of Sylvia Paine, my editor, who reigned in my lexical excesses, and is a fine person besides.Carol Evans-Smith and Ned Skubic did a fine design job in giving the book it's present look. Bob, Rick and Kathy at Graph-Tronics have been incredibly helpful throughout the production process.

The photos wouldn't have been complete without the swell props. John Quick at WCCO Radio loaned me Cedric Adam's mike. Susan Brady, Mitch Sondreal, Joanne Liebler, Nancy Anderson and everybody else who loaned me their funky snowshakers has my thanks. Cousin Becky, friends Katherine, Kathryn, and Sue brought their own logging equipment. Bill Andresen really distributes Lutefisk out of that truck, and Dana Ellavsky really is working her way through North Dakota State selling sweet corn.

Julie Ingebretsen and her husband Craig Bloomstrand have been absolutely invaluable to the marketing of this book. Linda Glenn is the greatest production supervisor a person could hope to have, and the contributions of John Dufresne, Jim Martin,and Byron Anderson have helped to make this book as swell as it is. Joan Siegel has been a superb source of advice and direction from the earliest stages of this book. Judy Olausen is one of the world's best photographers, and she still took my picture. Watch out - she's already in the next book as The Demon Who Made a Scene in Public! *Tusen tack* to Truda Stockenstrom for her hip, idiomatic Swedish translations. And what a debt of gratitude I owe to Pam Eyden, who threw the party where the idea for the book first took root.

Finally, and most importantly, I want to thank my Sweetie, Adaire, for putting up with the craziness and still loving me. Thanks as well to my mother, Dorothy Oas/Anderson/Kiser, who still - occasionally - doesn't know what to make of me, and my dad, Ralph William Anderson, who should be here to see this, since I am copying his sense of humor.

Why not share the giggles,
guffaws and general goofiness of
SCANDINAVIAN HUMOR & OTHER MYTHS
with your friends?

$10.95 (Mailing & handling included)

MAIL TO: Nordbook
　　　　　P.O.Box 6456
　　　　　Minneapolis, MN 55406
Minnesota Residents
please add 6% sales tax

I have enclosed$_____for _____books.

Name _____

Address_____

City_____ State_____ Zip_____

MAIL TO: Nordbook
　　　　　P.O.Box 6456
　　　　　Minneapolis, MN 55406
Minnesota Residents
please add 6% sales tax

I have enclosed$_____for _____books.

Name _____

Address_____

City_____ State_____ Zip_____